to Andrea
Love, Pop

Ways to Pray

Growing Closer to God

WAYS TO PRAY

Growing Closer to GOD

Cardinal Donald Wuerl

Our Sunday Visitor Publishing Division
Our Sunday Visitor, Inc.
Huntington, Indiana 46750

19 18 17 16 15 1 2 3 4 5 6 7 8 9

Our Sunday Visitor Publishing Division
Our Sunday Visitor, Inc.
200 Noll Plaza
Huntington, IN 46750
1-800-348-2440

ISBN: 978-1-61278-846-3 (Inventory No. T1648)
eISBN: 978-1-61278-850-0
LCCN: 2015953959

Cover design: Amanda Falk
Cover image: Shutterstock

Printed in the United States of America

Contents

CHAPTER 1

Prayer in the Air

Frequent flyers know the advantages of aisle seats on long flights. The position makes it easier to stand and stretch your legs without disturbing others. The open area beside you gives a little more room to maneuver if you want to retrieve papers from your briefcase.

For a priest, there are other advantages as well. A clergyman visible — on a plane, in an airport, or anywhere, really — is a clergyman available. People see a Roman collar, and they know they can approach its wearer with questions about the most personal and important things, about matters of the spirit.

My ticket directed me to such a seat on a flight late in 2013. The flight attendant greeted me as she went about her routines to prepare for takeoff, and she even stopped to introduce herself. She seemed happy to have a Catholic priest there among her passengers.

When the plane reached its cruising altitude, the captain granted us our freedom to move about, and she made her way quickly to the aisle space by my seat. After some customary pleasantries, she crouched down so that she was speaking at my level. "Do you mind if I ask a few questions?" she asked.

"Not at all," I replied.

She seemed not to care about the discomfort of sitting in the aisle. She told me her story. She had been raised in a nominally Catholic home. Her parents weren't churchgoers, but they cared enough about the faith to send their daughter to a Catholic school for the first few years of her education. She remembered those years as a peaceful time, and she attributed that sense to the routines of prayer that defined those early-childhood school days.

While still very young, however, she transferred to another school, and her life went on. She did the things she was supposed to do. She went to college, fell in love, and married a good man. She enjoyed her work for the airline. Yet she felt something was missing — something important — and when she looked back on her life, she longed for the sense of wholeness she knew when she was a student in Catholic school.

I asked her if she prayed. She said that she didn't even remember how to pray.

"Yes, you do," I assured her. I reminded her that the basic prayers in the tradition were the Sign of the Cross, the Lord's Prayer ("Our Father"), the Hail Mary, and the Glory Be.

She said she remembered the names of the prayers, but not the words. "The words will come back," I assured her, "as soon as you start to say the prayers."

Her eyes lit up. "Oh, could we say them now?"

So we did. We prayed, right there at the intersection of aisle and row on a great jetliner. She stumbled over words now and then, but I could see the recognition and remembrance play out in her expressions as she followed me through a slow recitation of the prayers.

In the end she radiated pure joy. She thanked me — but she didn't get up. She went on to say: "I wish I could pray this way with my husband." I assured her that she could; but she said he had had no religious upbringing whatsoever.

"Then you'll teach him to pray," I said, "and that's where it will begin."

"Oh, I couldn't do that. You saw that I barely know the prayers myself."

I reached in my briefcase and pulled out a devotional magazine. In the back were the texts of all the prayers, printed on a single page. I tore out the page and handed it to her. "Now you have everything you need. Pray these with your husband."

She looked at me as if I had handed her the deed to her dream home. Perhaps I had.

It's a conversation that recurs in human history. It's a conversation that recurs throughout our lives.

Jesus was praying in a certain place, when one of his disciples said to him, "Lord, teach us to pray, as John taught his disciples" (Luke 11:1). It is an important question, and even an urgent one. Maybe the disciple felt sheepish about bothering the great Master about such a simple matter. But he got over his inhibitions, because he *needed* to know how to pray.

We all do. We need to learn how to pray, and we need to spend our lives at that task. There's no graduation ceremony this side of the grave.

In our time on earth we must learn to speak the language of heaven. We must grow accustomed to God's constant, intimate presence. In heaven that experience will not require effort; but here on earth we need to work at it. Prayer is a gift from God — a grace — but God wants us to unwrap the gift and freely put it to use. God is sovereign, and no one can really force his hand, but he does want us to apply ourselves to prayer with diligence, passion, focus, and endurance — all the virtues we marshal when we pursue something we value. People are willing to work hard and sacrifice for the sake of family, career, education, and health. We should be far more eager to learn to pray well. As our flight attendant learned through her own experience, the ability (or inability) to pray affects our capacity to enjoy everything else in life.

What, then, is prayer?

This is not a trick question. Prayer is one of those basic realities — like *light*, *air*, and *life* — that seem so familiar to us that they hardly need to be defined. Their meaning should be self-evident. Yet when we actually try to define any of these — light, air, life, or prayer — they resist simplification and summary.

The *Catechism of the Catholic Church* poses the question, and then proposes helpful, if quite diverse, answers from the saints, who are authorities on the subject.

The classic formula comes from St. John of Damascus, who wrote in the eighth century: "Prayer is the raising of one's mind and heart to God or the requesting of good things from God" (see CCC 2559). This definition has endured so long because it sums up a complex and multifaceted activity.

Prayer, as St. John indicates, is a transcendent act. It is a "raising" of our faculties above their natural objects and ordinary inclinations. We transcend what is earthly by lifting up our minds and hearts to God. This does not mean that our souls are whisked out of our bodies in a mystical ecstasy; nor does it mean that we become forgetful or negligent of our earthly concerns and those of our friends. If we have these matters in mind when we pray, or if they're weighing on our heart, then we lift them up to God.

St. John adds, almost as an afterthought, a secondary definition of prayer: "the requesting of good things from God." It is a necessary part of the definition; but it is interesting that St. John chose to present it in the second place. Perhaps he was trying to adjust some commonplace notions about prayer.

It's true, after all, that we are more likely to pray when we want or need something. We are far less likely to "raise mind and heart" when things are going well. We're too busy enjoying ourselves! The stark example of this is in chapter 17 of St. Luke's Gospel. Ten lepers stood at a distance and cried out for Jesus to have mercy and heal them. They were living in physical pain and social isolation. Their needs were overwhelming. Their prayer was urgent. Jesus heard them, and he gave them exactly what they asked. Yet only *one* of those ten lepers made the effort to return to Jesus and say, "Thank you."

It is a common human temptation to reduce prayer to mere asking — not praising, not thanking, not confessing sins, but just asking for things. Even devout Christians can fall into the habit of listing off their "intentions" in their time of prayer. The English word *prayer* itself witnesses to this tendency. In ordinary usage, long ago, "to pray" simply meant to *ask*, *beg*, or *implore*. The word applied not only to petitions before heaven, but mostly to simple requests made from one person to another. In the play *Romeo and Juliet*, one of the characters wants to escape the midday heat, so he says to his companion: "I pray thee, good Mercutio, let's retire." At some point, English speakers came to equate "prayer" with "begging from God."

But prayer — St. John of Damascus would have us know — is much more than just asking God for something. Prayer is more than a pious filling out of an order form. It's an activity that involves all our faculties — our intellect, will, affections, and even our bodies. Prayer lifts us up, and brings about an intimate personal relationship between the God who made us and ourselves.

It's important for us to note that St. John does not dismiss or belittle our very real needs. He recognizes that prayers of petition are important. In fact, they help us to remember our neediness before God. Nevertheless, they are not the only form of prayer or the most important form.

If we want to have a satisfying life of prayer — if we want to grow in the spiritual life — we need to do more when we pray than beg favors. We need to build a relationship.

Alongside St. John's definition of prayer, the *Catechism of the Catholic Church* presents a more modern offering from St. Thérèse of Lisieux, who lived at the end of the nineteenth century. Her definition is intense, personal, and dynamic. "For me, prayer is a surge of the heart," she wrote. "It is a simple look turned toward heaven, it is a cry of recognition and of love, embracing both trial and joy."

St. Thérèse's definition implies a relationship that is already well developed. Only with those who know us well can we communicate with "a simple look" turned in their direction. St. Thérèse enjoyed a deep intimacy with God, and that is evident in the way she described prayer. Yet she did not think that such intimacy should be exceptional. She wrote as if the "surge of the heart" and the "simple look" were forms of prayer that we might all enjoy.

So how does an ordinary person get there? Unlike young Thérèse, most of us live in neighborhoods, not monasteries. Our days are busy with many things: voice mails, e-mails, driving, meetings, appointments, paying bills, and fulfilling obligations. Where does prayer fit in the mix? How much prayer and how often? What kinds of prayer?

The Catholic tradition offers us many ways to approach those questions. Our heritage is rich in forms and styles of prayer. We have so much to choose from that the choice can seem overwhelming. This book is designed to make the beginnings of prayer less intimidating. In the opening chapters we'll examine the different categories of prayer, some basic terms of prayer, and the qualities we should look for in our prayer. Then we'll briefly consider the values of planning, routine, and habit as they relate to our dealings with God. At the heart of the book we'll look at the prayers themselves in their very catholic (universal) variety. We'll explore their meaning, their history, and quite practically how to pray them.

This book is an exercise we can undertake together. For prayer is like exercise, a basic human need that does not go away. What's more, in prayer we must always strive to move forward, or we'll fall woefully behind. Think of St. Paul. He was admirably educated, well practiced, and even divinely inspired as an Apostle. He was a founder of churches, a bishop, and a teacher and preacher of prayer. Yet even he had to admit "we do not know how to pray as we ought" (Romans 8:26).

To make such an admission is to take the first step forward. And so, on good authority, we begin.

CHAPTER 2

Where Prayer Begins

Prayer is primary, said Pope Francis in one of his early homilies as pope. "The first task in life is this: prayer."[1]

He went on to describe prayer as an act with three movements: "gazing on the Lord, hearing the Lord, asking the Lord."

His words seem simple; but on reflection they are quite provocative. In his brief analysis, the Holy Father manages to upset some of the most common notions about prayer.

No one would dispute with him over the elements in his sequence: gazing, hearing, and asking. Those are basic components in most of our everyday conversations, and prayer (according to St. Teresa of Ávila) is nothing more than conversation with God. We observe good manners when we look in the direction of the people with whom we're speaking, when we listen to them, and when we speak to those whose company we share.

But notice the sequence in the pope's instruction: "hearing" comes before "asking." He tells us to begin by gazing in God's direction, but the next step is not talking. It's "hearing" — listening. It's receiving a word that is given.

Even our gaze, it seems, is turned toward Someone who is waiting for us, Someone who has first called us.

The initiative in prayer, then, is not ours. It is God's, and it was taken a long time ago.

God formed us from the womb, and he knew us before he formed us (see Jeremiah 1:5; Isaiah 44:2). In all relations between earth and heaven, the Almighty has taken the initiative. He has begun the conversation.

From the beginning of the Scriptures — from the beginning of creation — it is clear that human beings were created for intimacy with God. In the first chapter of the Book of Genesis we see God fashioning the world, the stars, the moon, and the animals, and he establishes the laws of their nature. But the creation of man and woman is essentially different from God's other actions. He made Adam and Eve "in his own image" (Genesis 1:27) — and he spoke to them directly (Genesis 1:28–30). He didn't merely program laws for human instinct, as he had done for the animals, or set the course of gravity, as he had done for the planets and stars. He began a conversation. He called out to man and woman, and he awaited a response. God "walked" in the garden where they lived (Genesis 3:8). There was no obstacle in the conversation between the human couple and the Lord God because they were sinless. They were "not ashamed" (Genesis 2:25).

Shame is an impediment to any conversation. It impedes relationship. Remember that Pope Francis' sequence of prayer began with "gazing." If we are ashamed, if we feel guilty, we cannot bear the gaze of someone who knows our faults. We find it difficult to make eye contact. When Adam and Eve disobeyed God, they could not bear to have intimate conversation with him. They hid from his presence.

Yet, even then, God continued to call out to them, with question after question. Why did God ask questions? He did not need to discover anything. God is all-knowing.

He asked questions so that Adam and Eve might respond — so that they might pray!

Even when the first couple had shattered their bond with God, he sought right away to restore it. He invited them to talk. The initiative was his, not theirs. God called first.

That remained the pattern through all of sacred history. Abram was an old man going about his business in the city of Ur when God called him to inhabit a faraway land and become father of a great nation (Genesis 12:1–2). In a similar way, many centuries later, God called to Moses from a burning bush (Exodus 3:1–6). One by one, the prophets of the Old Testament arise — not because they decided that prophet would be an interesting or lucrative career path — but because God first called them.

The human response to God's call is always halting, intermittent, and imperfect, because our sin holds us back. That's what St. Paul meant in the line we quoted in the last chapter: "we do not know how to pray as we ought" (Romans 8:26). In falling from grace, the human race has fallen out of practice in the art of prayer.

In his mercy, God assumed our human nature in Jesus Christ, so that we might learn from him how to pray. Jesus' whole life is a perfect prayer to God. His relationship is one of unbroken communion with the Father. When the Word became flesh (John 1:14), he showed us how we should conduct our prayer lives.

Thus, Jesus is the model and the teacher of prayer. He gives instruction in the fine points of prayer, and he shows us by example how to follow through. The disciples first see Jesus at prayer, and then they want to pray as he does, so they ask him how to do it.

The four Gospels record the testimony of eyewitnesses to the life of Jesus, and they show us a man who prayed often and prayed in many different ways. In the synagogues he joined in the public prayer — the liturgy — of the Jewish people (Luke 4:16; 13:10). He also prayed alone on mountaintops or in other deserted places (Mark 6:46). He gave thanks before sharing meals with people (Matthew 15:36). He prayed from Scripture, using the Psalms (Matthew 27:46, citing Psalm 22:1), and he prayed spontaneously from his heart (Luke 10:21). He made pilgrimage to Jerusalem on the feast days prescribed by the Law of Moses (John 2:23). He prayed before the most important acts and decisions of his ministry (Luke 6:12). At times, it seems, he prayed to recover his strength and energy (Mark 1:35).

This is the model life of prayer. If we want to succeed at the task, we should devote careful attention to the Master's pattern of living as well as to his teaching. Both the lifestyle and the words of Jesus show that prayer should have an important place in the life of every Christian. The rhythm of Jesus' life should be the rhythm of our own. Read the end of the opening chapter of St. Mark's Gospel, from verse 33 on. Jesus works intensely — teaching, healing, casting out demons, ministering to great crowds of people. Then he goes away "to a lonely place" to pray — and then he repeats the cycle of work and prayer.

That is the rhythm God created for us to keep. Jesus restored the cycle that Adam and Eve had broken through their sin. When we follow Jesus in our life of prayer, we begin to restore the balance, peace, and wholeness that God intends for our lives.

God created us. He sustains us in life, and he saves us from our sins. At every stage, the relationship of prayer begins with God's invitation. Sometimes we can identify God's action quite clearly as an intervention. Think of those paintings that show St. Paul bathed in heavenly light as he's knocked to the ground.

Other times, however, God's action is quite subtle. Ignatius of Loyola was annoyed and bored because he was confined to his sickbed, but had run out of adventure stories to read. So, in desperation, he reached for a book he would not ordinarily have read: a collection of stories about the saints. And God reached him through those stories — moved him to conversion and inspired him to found the Jesuit order.

The first move always belongs to God. Then he awaits our response in prayer.

Yet even in waiting he is working. Remember St. Paul's observation that "we do not know how to pray as we ought"? Well, God will not allow us to remain in helpless ignorance. Again, he makes the first move and sends the Holy Spirit to live in us — and pray in us. "The Spirit himself intercedes for us with sighs too deep for words" (Romans 8:26). "When we cry, 'Abba! Father!' it is the Spirit himself bearing witness with our spirit that we are children of God" (Romans 8:15–16).

God does the calling. God makes the invitation. He initiates the relationship of prayer. If we can respond at all, it is because he is responding in us, as a parent might help a toddler child to finish a sentence.

To pray this way is true conversation with God. But, like any loving conversation — like any meeting of friends or spouses — prayer is more than a mere exchange of words and ideas. It is a true sharing of life. St. Peter says that by saving us God has empowered us to "become partakers of the divine nature" (2 Peter 1:4).

That's prayer! To share God's life. To speak with the Holy Spirit. To imitate Jesus Christ. To call God "Father" — and mean it!

To pray, then, is to enjoy a life that has been raised as high as a life can go.

We could never aspire to anything so good. God had to *invite* us and then make it possible for us to respond.

Nevertheless, our response must be free. Otherwise it could not be a response of genuine love. True love cannot be coerced. God could not just program it mechanically into our nature. He wants us to give ourselves willingly, expressing our love in our prayer and actions, as Jesus did throughout his earthly life.

We think of prayer as something we give to God, and so it is. But it always begins as something God gives to us.

He has started the conversation for us, by means of his grace. But he continues the conversation, even today, through the same methods of prayer that Jesus used. We find them well tended in the Catholic tradition. In every age, Christians have attended the Church's public liturgy — and practiced private meditation. We have, like Jesus, prayed the traditional blessing before meals. We pray spontaneously. We pray the Psalms. We pray alone, and we pray with family, friends, and neighbors.

All of these ways will be beneficial to us. Our challenge is to do them all in the right proportion, do them well, and do them faithfully over time.

That should be our goal as we go forward in this book. We'll examine the various forms of prayer and consider how they might fit into an overarching program for our spiritual life. Maybe that sounds unusual or intimidating, but it's not. It's simply doing for our relationship with God what we would do for any other human relationship. When life gets busy, it's difficult for friends to remain friendly without some level of planning and effort. It's difficult for parents to stay close to their children — or spouses to stay close to one another — if they don't make opportunities for conversation.

We want our bonds to grow stronger over time. We want our relationships to grow closer. The ordinary way this happens is through talking and listening. We make time for one another, and we proceed to fill that time in a variety of meaningful ways. We exchange customary greetings. We exchange updates, concerns, ideas, hopes, wishes, plans, fears. This is how we share life with one another. We take what's inside us — what is entirely interior — and we communicate it to another person. At the same time, we make the effort to hear, understand, and respond to the other person.

We know this process from everyday life. God wants us to learn how the same dynamic — the same habits and customs — apply to our friendship with him. That's why he has called us to prayer, you and me, since the dawn of creation.

CHAPTER 3

The Habit of Prayer

Sargent Shriver was a great statesman and humanitarian. He won renown as the founder of the Peace Corps and the architect of the social programs of President Lyndon Johnson. He served as the U.S. ambassador to France. He ran for vice-president in 1972. A detailed resume of his career could fill a book.

He was also a man of habitual prayer, faithful to his daily devotions throughout his lifetime. It wasn't his accomplishments or social status that defined Sargent Shriver. His son Mark said it well: "Going to Mass daily, having a daily relationship with God, even a minute-by-minute relationship with God — that's what gave Dad 'power,' gave him his hope."[2]

All of his political accomplishments were in the distant past in 2010 when I saw him brought, in a wheelchair, to the front of St. Matthew's Cathedral in Washington, D.C. He was there for our first-ever archdiocesan "White Mass," celebrated for people with disabilities and their caregivers. With his wife, Eunice Kennedy Shriver, "Sarge" had long been an advocate for this particular cause. Now he was himself severely disabled, ninety-five years old and suffering from dementia, at an advanced stage of Alzheimer's disease. Not only were his professional and personal achievements receding into the past, he had lost his memories of most of them.

Yet he remembered everything about the Mass. Again, here is his son's description, from his bestselling memoir, *A Good Man*: "When he was supposed to stand, he stood; when he was supposed to kneel, he knelt; when he was supposed to bless himself, he did."[3]

Sargent Shriver had done so much in life, but he had always made time for Mass — every day. Bit by bit, he lost possession of everything he had, but his habitual experience of the Mass remained with him. It was so deeply ingrained that it was practically ineradicable; and he was able to draw comfort and joy from it (and from the Rosary) as his life drew to a close.

Such is the force of habit. Such is the power of spiritual discipline. Sargent Shriver lived his spiritual life according to a program, a plan. That was a challenge, I'm sure, when he was working long hours in the White House and in an embassy; but the benefits, for himself and for his family, were incalculable.

Habit and discipline don't often get the credit they deserve, especially in spiritual matters. Popular culture today prizes variety over regularity, improvisation over formula, and spontaneity over routine. Many people say that they're "spiritual, but not religious" — meaning that they'd rather not make the kind of commitments that religion has always demanded. "Spiritual" — apart from religion — becomes a vague term suggestive of indeterminate beliefs loosely held, always subject to change, manifest more in emotions than in practices.

The problem with such an approach is that it lacks the power to form a life, as Catholicism formed Sargent Shriver's. "Spiritual, but not religious" is not an approach that can inspire great cathedrals or great civilizations. It doesn't give us anything solid to cling to when everything else is slipping away from us.

The word *religious* comes from the Latin word for "binding." We grow spiritually as we bind our lives to Christ, and we make that bond stronger through the force of our habits of prayer.

This should come as no surprise to us. Though Americans say they value improvisation, variety, and spontaneity, we really do prefer to patronize pharmacists, doctors, and other professionals who follow routines and stick to the formulas. We expect musicians and athletes to practice before they perform for us.

We all acknowledge that the truly important things in life shouldn't be left to improvisation. And our relationship with God is, truly, the most important thing in life. Spontaneity plays a part in it; but we must not leave it entirely to the ups and downs of our emotions and our energy level. Spontaneity itself arises from accustomed patterns, acquired by repeated practice. Musicians excel at improvisation only after they've gained mastery of their scales and chords.

We need to build up our prayer the way we would build up our muscles, through a regular program of spiritual "exercises" that become habitual. In the Catholic tradition, this is known as a "program of life" or "plan of life."

Monasteries follow such a plan. Monks and nuns pray the Psalms at appointed hours; attend Mass at a certain time; take their meals together; gather for shared community reading; and so on. The schedule is fixed by the community's superiors.

Laypeople and parish priests often require more flexibility in their daily rounds, to accommodate the unpredictability of life in the world. Nevertheless, our resolution to pray *at regular times* should be firm. The contemporary spiritual writer Fr. Michael Scanlan, T.O.R., called our times of prayer "appointments with God," and he insisted that we should *keep* our appointments.

> What does it mean to have an appointment? It means you set aside a time and place to be with someone. It means you make some kind of commitment to be somewhere at such and such an hour, at such and such a place to meet with so and so.[4]

Whenever we make an appointment, we are making a commitment involving a time, a place, and a person or persons. People are depending on us. We want to be dependable.

If we believe in God, we know that no one on earth should be more important to us. No professional or personal relationship should take priority over the time we commit to spend with our Creator and Redeemer, our Lord and Giver of Life. We should keep this fact in mind as we begin to sketch out a plan of life — as we begin to set the appointments we intend to keep, day after day, for as many days as God gives us.

Jesus preached a parable that's applicable to our consideration of time management.

> A man going on a journey called his servants and entrusted to them his property; to one he gave five talents, to another two, to another one, to each according to his ability. Then he went away. He who had received the five talents went

> at once and traded with them; and he made five talents more. So also, he who had the two talents made two talents more. But he who had received the one talent went and dug in the ground and hid his master's money (Matthew 25:14–18).

You know the rest of the story. The Master was pleased with those who invested his money well and earned a profit. He grew furious with the lazy servant who buried his talent in a field.

Time is the great treasure God has given us. How much of it have we returned to him for his investment? How much time have we set aside so that we can praise him, thank him, ask his forgiveness, and petition him on behalf of others? If we don't reserve the time in advance, we're unlikely to find it as we fly from one preoccupation to another.

What preoccupies us is important and often urgent, but our response even to those alarms will be better if we respond fresh from our daily prayer. We will learn to see difficulties from God's perspective. We will learn to approach our challenges in the light of the Holy Spirit. We will begin to see other people as God sees them. Regular prayer will, no doubt, benefit us in the natural order as well as the supernatural.

But we get the benefits only if we make the commitment — only if we resolve to make a plan, make it specific, and then stick with it over the long haul.

I've noted that prayer is like exercise. Prayer is also like food. Just as the body needs nourishment in order to live, so does the soul. Prayer is the food of the soul.

We Americans pride ourselves on our eclectic cuisine, our heart-smart diets, and our artful arrangement of flavors, textures, and colors at mealtime. Most homes, I would wager, have more than one cookbook. The kitchen is the residence of many of our major appliances.

We put effort into our meals; we plan ahead for them; and we tend to show up for them on time. We do this because food is important to us. We appreciate it for its flavor and nutrition. If we're late for a meal — or if we skip a meal — we feel it. Our blood sugar drops. We get fatigued and irritable.

When we skip our prayer or skimp on our prayer, something similar happens. Our sense of God's presence grows dull; so does our ability to see Christ in others; so does our moral sense. Circumstances weary us. We get irritable.

With a good plan of life, we can enjoy a healthy spiritual life, as varied and enjoyable as a good diet. The Catholic tradition gives us so much to work with — many types and forms of prayer, which we'll examine more closely in the chapters to come.

Jesus said that we "ought always to pray and not lose heart" (Luke 18:1). "Always" doesn't mean that we will spend every waking moment saying prayers and attending devotions. It means that we will learn to turn our life into prayer.

We cannot do that, however, until we have seasoned our entire day with periods of prayer that are deliberate and attentive. We need to make prayer a habit.

In Catholicism, *habit* is a word rich in suggestive power. There is what we might call its common meaning: a habit is simply a firm and stable pattern of behavior. A habit is a disposition to do certain things with ease, to act the same way in a given circumstance. What is habitual does not require a lot of forethought.

Habit can also refer to the distinctive clothing worn by a monk, nun, or member of a religious order. We "wear" our habits, and they distinguish us from others. They identify us as members of God's family.

The word is the foundation of many other English words as well, words like *habitat* and *habitation* — words that mean "environment" and "home." Our habits are where we live, where we choose to spend our time. We should indeed grow to feel at home in them.

All these modern terms come from an ancient Latin root, the word *habere*, which means to *have*, *hold*, *possess*, and *keep*.

By itself the word *habit* is neutral, and can be used to describe good patterns (which we call virtues) or bad patterns (which we call vices). The word is neutral, but in life our habits will always fall into one category or another. And no matter how much we say we value spontaneity, our lives will settle into one kind of pattern or another.

We want our habits to be virtuous. We want to be remembered for virtue. We want to live off the strength of our God-given virtue, even when we can no longer remember our virtuous acts.

Habit is acquired through repeated acts. By our plan of life we set our course for virtue. We correct our course daily. We do this habitually, but not in a mindless way. Prayer is not a rote or knee-jerk response. We take up our task daily, as the patriarch Jacob did in the Old Testament (Genesis 29), and fulfill it dutifully, but entirely for the sake of love.

CHAPTER 4

Types of Prayer

Msgr. Tran Ngoc Thu had a challenging job.[5] A priest from Vietnam, he was invited in 1988 to serve as personal secretary to Pope John Paul II. The globetrotting pope was arguably the busiest man on earth at the time.

Every pope must fill a variety of roles. He is shepherd to a billion Catholics spread over all the inhabited continents. As Vicar of Christ, he must teach his flock unceasingly by his writings, preaching, and personal presence. The pope is also temporal ruler of the Vatican City State, and so he must oversee a diplomatic corps, banking system, and all the usual sort of public works and utilities. Pope St. John Paul II applied himself to all of these tasks with intensity and focus.

But he did still more. He traveled more than any of his predecessors. He wrote more — letters, books, articles, private messages. He met with more people, receiving dozens into his apartment for his "private" Masses and hundreds into the audience hall after his Wednesday addresses.

Msgr. Tran Ngoc Thu's job was to make sure that the pontiff stayed on schedule and that all the tasks got done. His work was made more difficult by the fact that he couldn't speak or understand a word of Polish, the pope's native language. He learned, by necessity, to be very attentive to the Holy Father's actions.

And what did he notice? He found that as much as St. John Paul was a man of action — extraordinary action, prodigious action — he was still more a man of prayer. His day was defined not so much by the rush of activity as by the constancy of prayer.

St. John Paul was a towering intellectual figure, one of the most renowned academic philosophers of his day. So we might imagine that his prayer was meditative and high-flown; and, according to Msgr. Tran, we would be correct. Shortly after rising at 5:30 a.m., the pope would go to the chapel and kneel on the bare floor (at least in those younger years) and would bury his head in his hands. It was as if he was pressing his brilliant mind to the infinite mind of God.

John Paul was a great intellectual, but his prayer was not just an intellectual matter. His secretary noticed that the Holy Father also remained faithful to the common devotions he had learned as a little child from his parents. He was especially fond of the Rosary and somehow managed to pray the beads several times a day. If he experienced delays, he filled the unexpected downtime with decades of the Rosary, fitting in as much of it as he could. He also prayed the Church's traditional noontime prayer, the Angelus of Our Lady. Wherever he was working, at home or abroad, he made periodic brief "visits" to Jesus, present in the tabernacle of a nearby church. Every Friday he prayed the Stations of the Cross. Every Saturday he went to Confession. He offered up any suffering, discomfort, or disappointment that came his way. He spent long stretches kneeling before the tabernacle interceding with Jesus for people worldwide who had written to ask for his prayers. He also prayed the Divine Office, the traditional daily prayer — mostly Psalms and readings — offered by priests and religious. Most importantly, every day he celebrated the Holy Sacrifice of the Mass.

Just scanning Monsignor's list of devotions, we might think that the pope did nothing but pray! The truth, however, is that most of those periods of devotion were brief, and they provided respite from hours of intense labor — meetings, drafting documents, reviewing documents, revising documents, studying budgets, taking phone calls, attending meetings, and initialing and signing hundreds of sheets of paper per day. Through many of the hours of most of his days, St. John Paul did the work of a typical executive or administrator.

Very few people will face responsibilities on that grand scale. Yet all of us would like to go about our tasks with the same kind of serenity, attention, and effectiveness as St. John Paul did. We would like to have access to the same range of religious expression, from heartfelt petition to awestruck adoration, from genuine sorrow to joyful thanksgiving.

He kept it all together because he followed a plan of life. His prayer was anything but boring or monotonous, because in his plan he made a place for many different kinds of prayer. You and I can draw our practices of prayer from the same treasury as St. John Paul. We have access to the same great tradition, with all its immense and amazing variety.

We should be dazzled by the richness of the prayers employed by St. John Paul, and I hope you will be dazzled as we look more closely at each of the Church's particular devotions. It will be helpful, however, if we look first at the broad, general categories the Church uses to classify all of these many pious practices. John Paul chose judiciously from each category, finding the balance that was right for him and eminently doable even in his busy days. As we begin to make our own plan, we should seek to do the same.

Traditionally the Church has referred to four general types of prayer: adoration, thanksgiving, petition, and contrition. We should find a place in our plan for each type.

1. Adoration is the purest form of prayer. It is prayer that glorifies God not because of *what he does* for us, but for *who he is* in himself. Adoration is sometimes expressed as praise. When we are moved by wonder or awe — by a scene of natural beauty, for example, a mountain or a mighty river — we can praise the God who created all that we see. In the Bible, such adoration is often expressed in the word Hallelujah — Alleluia — which is Hebrew for "Praise the Lord."

When we praise God, as when we praise other people, it is good for us to be as specific as possible. "I praise you, Lord, for the seeming miracle of a newborn baby." "I praise you for your mighty deeds in history. You always save your people." It's not that God needs our compliments. God is entirely self-sufficient. But the effort is good for us. Specific praise makes for a stronger prayer life, just as it makes for a stronger marriage or managerial style.

Adoration should be our primary attitude before God. As we begin to pray, we should recognize where we stand in our relationship. And so we acknowledge that he is our Creator, and we are his creatures. This attitude is evident in so many of the Psalms:

> O come, let us worship and bow down,
> let us kneel before the LORD, our Maker!
> For he is our God,
> and we are the people of his pasture,
> and the sheep of his hand. (Psalm 95:6–7)

To pray this Psalm is to speak with profound humility and yet deep joy and confidence.

Our tradition offers us many examples of prayers of Adoration. There are, for example, the Divine Praises we recite at Benediction: "Blessed be God. Blessed be his holy name. Blessed be Jesus Christ, true God and true man…." Many of the most popular hymns also express praise for the Almighty: "Holy God, We Praise Thy Name" and "How Great Thou Art" come immediately to mind.

2. Thanksgiving is closely related to adoration. It is an expression of gratitude for the spiritual and material gifts God has given us. Prayers of praise naturally lead us to thank God, because he has used his might and his goodness for our benefit.

Jesus always remembered to give thanks before he "broke bread." He did this at the multiplication of loaves and fishes. He did it also at the Last Super, when he took bread and wine and established the Eucharist. In fact, the word Eucharist itself comes from the Greek word for thanksgiving, *eucharistia*.

Even today, the most common Catholic prayer of thanksgiving is "Grace before Meals": "Bless us, O Lord, and these thy gifts, which we are about to receive from thy bounty through Christ our Lord. Amen." It is an ancient prayer, dating back at least to the fourth century, though it seems to have been well established by then.

Jesus did not limit his thanks to meals, however, and neither should we. He expressed gratitude especially for spiritual gifts, special graces, and the revelation of the Father (see Matthew 11:25). When we experience any joy, we should remember to thank God, because all joys come from God. To say "thank you" is simply good manners.

Thanksgiving is good for us because it reminds us that we are always on the receiving end of God's grace. When we say "thank you," we remember who we are in relation to God — and that is our deepest identity. When we say "thank you," we remember that we are God's children.

3. Petition — the prayer of request — is probably the form of prayer that's most commonly used. We tend to turn to God especially when we want something. This is not a bad thing. Our wants themselves are providential reminders of our dependence on God. Children petition their parents often because the things they want are beyond their reach, because they have few resources of their own, and because they have only a limited understanding of the world and how it works. Their circumstances constantly lead them to acknowledge their dependence on mom or dad.

Well, we too wish for things we cannot reach on our own. We too have paltry resources. We too can draw from a limited understanding of the world. All of our needs and wants, then, should lead us to prayers of petition — and sooner rather than later.

Unfortunately, we too often turn to God only as the last resort, when we have exhausted our natural options and resources. Then we're displeased with God if we don't promptly get exactly what we have asked for. This is not the Christian attitude. Prayer is not a bargaining process whereby we offer God something in return for something. Prayer is our dialogue with a Father who loves us and will always give us what is best for us — what we truly need — though it may not always be what we want. Again, we can learn much about petition if we consider the typical conversations between small children and their parents.

Petition has its place, and it is an important place. Jesus himself told us: "Truly, truly I say to you, if you ask anything of the Father, he will give it to you in my name.... Ask, and you will receive, that your joy may be full" (John 16:23–24). This promise is fulfilled for every Christian who truly prays in Christ's name with a proper disposition and for something that will be helpful to eternal salvation. God is all-powerful, and God wants his children to have abundant and everlasting joy.

We must be confident in our petitions. God always hears our prayers. He knows how to give good things to his children (see Matthew 7:11). Sometimes, however, we ask for the wrong things. So what should we pray for?

The *Catechism of the Catholic Church* tells us that "Christian petition is centered on the desire and *search for the Kingdom to come*" (CCC 2632). This sets a certain order of priorities for our prayer. For some things we must pray ("Thy kingdom come. Thy will be done.... Deliver us from evil."). For other things, we are free to pray ("Please let my mother's blood test be negative."). In everything we petition, we should, like trusting children, seek the will of "Our Father."

A subcategory of petition is intercession — favors we ask on behalf of another person. We learn to do this from Jesus, who is the true intercessor with the Father. St. Paul calls Jesus the "one mediator" (1 Timothy 2:5), even as he instructs us to make Christ-like "supplications" and "intercessions" for everyone (1 Timothy 2:1). St. Paul was himself a great intercessor (2 Thessalonians 1:11) and was constantly begging the prayers of others (2 Thessalonians 3:1).

4. Contrition is the expression of sorrow for our sins.

We know, instinctively, that sin is the great obstacle to our prayer life. When Adam and Eve became aware of God's presence, they were ashamed of their disobedience; and so they hid themselves, as if anyone could hide from a God who is almighty and omnipresent.

In faith we know we live in God's presence, and so we are aware of our moral failures. We regret them, and we tell him so. Jesus praised the humble tax collector who beat his breast and said: "God, be merciful to me a sinner!" (Luke 18:13).

The Catholic tradition offers us many ways to express our sorrow. The simplest and most ancient form of this prayer is the phrase "Lord, have mercy." It appears often in Scripture, and we repeat it in the Mass. At Mass we also pray the *Confiteor*, which begins: "I confess to almighty God and to you, my brothers and sisters, that I have greatly sinned...."

Among the prayers we learn as children are those known as "Acts of Contrition." From the Sisters who taught me in grade school I learned one that began: "O my God, I am heartily sorry for having offended you...." This prayer, in many variations, still appears in basic Catholic prayer books today.

The most sublime and beautiful expression of prayerful contrition is the Sacrament of Reconciliation, also known as "Confession" or "Penance."

There are other ways to categorize our conversation with God. Sometimes it's helpful to consider prayer according to its form rather than its theme. In that case, we can divide our practices into three categories: vocal prayer, mental prayer, and liturgical prayer.

Vocal prayer usually refers to set forms that are recited aloud. The Lord's Prayer and the Hail Mary are common vocal prayers. The phrase can be deceptive, however, as we can just as easily, and just as fruitfully, pray those prayers silently. What we really mean by vocal prayer is a prayer that has an established verbal form.

Mental prayer, by contrast, is an interior prayer that can be more conversational. God knows our thoughts, and so we need not speak them aloud. We can address them to God directly. When we practice mental prayer, we devote time to thoughtful, usually silent, conversation with God.

Mental prayer can involve words or it can be wordless. St. John Vianney, a parish priest, once asked a parishioner what he prayed about when he sat in front of the church's tabernacle. The parishioner responded that he just looked at Jesus, who looked back. As old friends know — and as longtime spouses know — a conversation can move forward without the benefit of words, by means of expressions and glances.

Liturgical prayer includes all of the Church's official public forms of worship: the sacraments, especially the Mass, the blessings, and the biblical Psalms and canticles as they are arranged in the Divine Office.

These three categories are distinct, but not exclusive. All prayer involves the mind, so all prayer is — to some degree — mental prayer. And mental prayer itself can sometimes be "vocalized" and spoken aloud. St. John Paul's secretary, Monsignor Tran, observed that the pope would sometimes, in the midst of his silent intercessory prayer, call out: "Lord, have mercy!" or some other plea.

Prayer is difficult to categorize, as it is difficult to place individual prayers in a discrete category. The Mass includes all four thematic types of prayer (adoration, thanksgiving, petition, and contrition) as well as all three forms of prayer (vocal, mental, and liturgical). Yet it remains one prayer. The Our Father similarly involves three of the four thematic types and can work rather neatly as vocal, mental, or liturgical prayer.

So why do we bother dividing prayer into categories? Is it just an academic exercise?

No, the categories serve very useful and practical purposes. Consider an example.

The temptations that we face in life also tend to fall into categories. We call them the seven deadly sins: wrath, greed, sloth, pride, lust, envy, and gluttony. These are the bad habits that consistently trouble human beings.

Spiritual writers tell us that we can often find an antidote for particular temptations in a particular type of prayer. For example, many people struggle with disordered pride. They think about themselves above all, and they forget about God. They want to be humble, perhaps, but the virtue eludes them. They become proud even of their advance toward humility — and then they're back at square one.

A more effective way to learn humility is through prayers of praise and thanksgiving. These serve as regular reminders that God is great — and we are not God!

In a similar way, some people struggle with sins involving disordered bodily appetites. What they want is fundamentally good — something created by God — but they want what is not theirs by right. They want food, or property — or even a human body — that belongs to someone else, or they want too much of it.

It can be helpful for such people to praise God for the part of creation they find so powerfully attractive. In doing so, they immediately place the "forbidden fruit" in context — not denying its goodness, but seeing its goodness properly, in God's light.

All of the thematic types of prayer and forms of prayer should find their place in our plan of life. This doesn't mean we need to pray many hours per day, or learn seven different techniques of prayer. We do not need to quit our day job in order to pray as Christians.

What we see in the lives of saints like Pope John Paul II is that we can be still more effective, personally and professionally, when we pray in a more habitual way in the Catholic tradition.

CHAPTER 5

Grace with Meals

Mary's Gourmet Diner operated quietly for years, serving up meals noticed only by its customers in Winston-Salem, North Carolina. It was known locally for its sumptuous breakfasts and unusual omelet combinations.

In 2014, however, Mary's made international news because of its spiritual principles.

An observant customer noticed that she had received a fifteen-percent discount on her check. When she asked her waitress about it, she learned that the diner automatically granted the discount to anyone who was seen praying before eating. The customer promptly called in the story to a Christian radio station, and from there the Good News went out to the ends of the earth.

The tempest that followed was rather remarkable. It was surely the first time in history that "saying grace" consumed so many column inches in print media and so many hours of talk radio. Christians applauded. Atheists complained about discrimination.

Mary, the diner's manager, chuckled and surely enjoyed an uptick in business — for which I'm sure she gave thanks.

I bring this up not so that we can learn how to profit financially from our prayer. I tell the story — at the beginning of our consideration of individual devotions — because it shows that a little prayer can be a very big deal.

If you're new to the idea of daily prayer, grace at meals is a good place to begin, and there are many reasons why this is so.

The most practical reason is that the prayer benefits from its association with an appointment we are unlikely to miss. Most people, most days, sit down to eat at least two or three times a day. If we're late to our accustomed mealtime, our bodies let us know. Grace is a prayer that comes with a built-in alarm.

The meal may be a granola bar consumed on the bus, or a drive-through order from a fast-food restaurant, or one of those large platters at Mary's Gourmet Diner. It doesn't matter: one size of grace fits all. Once we have made a habit of saying grace, it's hard to do without it. Our meals don't seem right if we miss it; they don't *taste* right.

Grace truly changes the character of a meal. The simple prayer takes a common event — the satisfaction of a natural need — and elevates it to a supernatural level. When we pray, we remember God's presence; and we know that he is there to witness our conversation at table. Grace also gives us a heightened awareness of our food and companions *as gifts from God*. Our brief blessing can transform a mundane necessity into a spiritual joy.

I dare say that our mealtimes need to be transformed. They need to be recovered as sacred events. That's the way biblical religion has always understood the sharing of a meal. When Abraham received three visitors from heaven, he sat them down and served them dinner (Genesis 18:1–8). When Moses and the Israelites encountered God, they ate and drank with him (Exodus 24:11). Bible scholars tell us that St. Luke composed his Gospel as a sequence of banquet scenes — Jesus sharing a table with a variety of friends and acquaintances. Jesus spoke often of heaven as a festive banquet; and he gave the Church a meal, the Eucharist, as its principal reason for gathering.

God's chosen people, the Israelites, placed a premium value on mealtimes. Archaeologists have unearthed many prayers from the time of Jesus — and most of them are table blessings. What do we know for sure about the community that produced the Dead Sea Scrolls? They were diligent about grace at meals.

We, too, should be so diligent.

The Pew Research Center has, for many years, been conducting a study of America's religious attitudes and practices. One of the questions they ask people is: "How often do you say grace or give a blessing to God before you eat a meal?" Recently, forty-four percent of all respondents said they do so at least once a day; another ten percent said they say grace at least once or twice a week.

One of the men who worked with the study, David Campbell of the University of Notre Dame, identified table blessings as one of the most telling signs of a person's commitment of faith: "If I know that you are a grace-sayer on a regular basis, I actually know a lot about you," he said. "I can predict a lot of things about what you believe and what you might even do in your life. This is a pretty useful indicator of the level of an individual's own religiosity."[6]

Grace is that important, because meals mean something to human beings. They're not like feeding times for livestock. They are moments that build fellowship. And when we acknowledge God's presence, the bond is much stronger.

Why? Because we are less likely to act divisively when we know that God is part of the conversation. If we know that God is near, we're unlikely to gossip, break promises, divulge another person's secrets, or indulge in unfair criticism.

Saying grace prepares the way for better conversations — and a reduced chance of indigestion.

Grace makes a difference, and it signifies a difference. Professor Campbell is right about that. Nor is he the only one who will see our prayer for what it is. If we say grace publicly, in a restaurant or on a park bench, it makes a statement; it marks a commitment. Even if all we do is bow or make the Sign of the Cross, people know what we're about, and they know what we believe. Just by saying grace, we evangelize.

So what do we mean by grace?

It's just offering thanks. The word comes from the Latin word *gratias*, which means "thanks."

We're free to express our gratitude in any way we choose. Most people begin by making the Sign of the Cross. Then, if we wish, we can speak spontaneously, from the heart. We can speak in general terms or be specific. We can use the traditional form passed down through the centuries: "Bless us, O Lord, and these your gifts, which we are about to receive from your bounty, through Christ Our Lord. Amen."

We can even just bow our heads and offer our prayer in silence.

Some people bow again at the end of every meal and offer a second grace: "We give you thanks, almighty God, for these and all your benefits which we have received from your bounty through Christ Our Lord. Amen."

All we mean by "saying grace" is offering thanks and asking God's blessing.

Yet, again, it is a valuable prayer. How valuable? It's at least worth noting that Norman Rockwell's painting *Saying Grace* broke all records when it sold for $46 million in 2013. At the time, that was the most money ever spent for a painting by an American artist. It more than doubled the auction house's estimate. The painting features a boy praying with an elderly woman in a crowded restaurant.

"Grace before meals," said Blessed Mother Teresa of Calcutta, is one of the "small deliberate things" that help us to cultivate "silence of the heart and mind."[7] And that is one of the great benefits of Christian prayer.

CHAPTER 6

The Basic Prayers

Jacques Maritain was a well-known figure in Paris during the early twentieth century. Though trained as a scholar — an academic philosopher — he did not shy away from public debate. Maritain's byline appeared regularly on the opinion pages of the newspapers and in popular journals. When the conversation demanded a readable book, he could produce one quickly, on subjects ranging from art to international relations. He was a man about town, a lively voice in the great and contentious conversation at the heart of French culture.

Maritain was an adult convert to the faith, and his voice was distinctively Catholic. He was not shy about his faith, and he began his public lectures by praying one of the simple prayers that every Catholic child would know: the Hail Mary.

More famous in Paris, however, was the composer Erik Satie. A solitary and eccentric man, he had won world-wide renown for his short compositions. Considered bold and experimental when they first appeared, these works are still a standard part of a piano student's repertoire; and they have appeared in the soundtracks of more than a hundred movies.

Raised a Catholic, Satie had a troubled adult life and fell away from the practice of the faith. He was disappointed in love and never recovered from a youthful affair. He took to drinking heavily and using drugs. He kept company with the most famous artists of the Parisian *avant garde*. But he lived alone and allowed no one to enter his apartment, where he worked constantly and produced his masterpieces. His approach to art was playful and unserious, and in speech he was often irreverent.

Maritain and Satie seemed unlikely candidates for a deep friendship. They differed about the deepest matters. Yet they became friends — first because Maritain took the time to review Satie's work and find the serious motivation behind its apparent frivolity. From there they could proceed to a years-long conversation about spiritual matters.

In the 1920s Satie suffered the effects of his drinking and drug abuse. His liver began to fail and he grew steadily sicker. Though Satie's company was gradually less amusing, Maritain stayed with him, and their friendship deepened.

One day in 1925 Maritain received word through a mutual friend that Satie was in St. Joseph's Hospital, and he rushed there to see him. Satie was so pleased by the visit. Alone with Maritain, the composer said, "You know, I'm not so anti-God as all that," and he confessed that since his childhood he had not failed to begin his days with the Sign of the Cross.

Satie asked to see a priest, and he made his Confession and received Holy Communion. Maritain's lasting memory was of Satie reciting the Church's basic prayers with the religious sisters who ran the hospital. "Our Father, who art in heaven.... Hail Mary, full of grace.... Glory be to the Father and to the Son and to the Holy Spirit...."

Maritain continued his visits even as Satie passed in and out of consciousness. The philosopher prayed his Rosary so that the composer could join in as he was able. Satie was fully awake when a priest came to anoint him. He said to Maritain, "It's good to be together like this … especially when we're thinking the same thoughts."

Maritain agreed and went back to praying the basic prayers of the Church: Our Father.… Hail Mary.… Glory be.… Such were the last words that passed between these two great men — and improbable friends.[8] The basic prayers provided common ground where two very different people could "think the same thoughts."

I began this book by telling the story of my encounter with a flight attendant. She and I were very different people, fulfilling very different roles in life, and we had vastly different experiences of childhood and adulthood. Yet we, like those two long-ago Parisians, could find common spiritual ground in the basic prayers of the Catholic faith — prayers we had both learned when we were very young. We could make the Sign of the Cross, and we could pray the Our Father, the Hail Mary, and the Glory Be.

All of these prayers arose in the early Church. All have roots in Scripture and were beloved by the early Christians. All have developed over time to arrive at their current popular form. It will be helpful for us to look at the Church's foundational prayers, one by one, and understand their origins, purpose, and meaning.

The Sign of the Cross. It is a simple gesture. Using our right hand, we trace the shape of the cross over our upper body, from the forehead downward to the chest, and then from our left shoulder to our right. As we make the Sign, we say: "In the name of the Father and of the Son and of the Holy Spirit. Amen."

It takes just a few words, and yet this prayer encapsulates the whole of the faith. It professes God as a Trinity of Persons (Father, Son, and Holy Spirit) and yet one God (the singular "name"). It proclaims the atonement of Jesus Christ and our salvation through the image of the cross. The gesture itself traces the way God loved the human race, descending from heaven to earth and taking flesh, then ascending to heaven, taking our glorified human nature with him. That is why we conclude at the right shoulder, just as Jesus concluded his journey "at the right hand of the Father" in heaven.

The earliest Christians made the Sign often, though it seems they made it differently. They used their thumb to trace a small cross on the forehead. A second-century Christian named Tertullian said that believers of his time made the Sign to begin and end a prayer or to sanctify a common activity such as getting dressed and putting on shoes.

It was common Christian practice to begin one's day by making the Sign of the Cross, and it has remained so. The Protestant reformer Martin Luther grew up with it and kept it all his life. He instructed his followers to do the same. It was a habit Erik Satie learned in childhood and was never able to shake, even when he was far from the faith.

It is customary to begin and end a period of prayer by making the Sign of the Cross.

The Our Father. This is traditionally called the Lord's Prayer because Jesus gave it to us verbatim. He said "Pray then like this," and he recited the words:

Our Father who art in heaven,
Hallowed be thy name.
Thy kingdom come.

Thy will be done,
  On earth as it is in heaven.
Give us this day our daily bread;
And forgive us our trespasses,
  As we forgive those who trespass against us;
And lead us not into temptation,
But deliver us from evil. (Matthew 6:9–13)

We could not have more authoritative advice on the subject of prayer. The first Christians heeded Our Lord and made it their custom to recite the Lord's Prayer three times a day.[9] When the great teachers of the ancient Church wished to teach on the subject of prayer, they simply went line by line through the Our Father. Tertullian and Cyprian did this in North Africa, Origen in Egypt, and Cyril in Jerusalem. In later years, the great saints — from Thomas Aquinas to Pope John Paul II — would compose their own commentaries. These are easily accessible (many are posted online for free) and serve as excellent spiritual reading, shoring up the very foundations of our prayer life.

The Hail Mary. This prayer is sometimes formally called the Angelic Salutation, because it begins with words spoken by the Archangel Gabriel to the Virgin Mary, recorded in St. Luke's Gospel: "Hail, full of grace, the Lord is with you!" (Luke 1:28). The next line was spoken by Mary's kinswoman Elizabeth on learning that Mary was pregnant with the Savior: "Blessed are you among women, and blessed is the fruit of your womb!" (Luke 1:42).

Already in the first millennium, Christians had the custom of addressing the Blessed Virgin with these lines. St. Peter Chrysologus, in the fifth century, illuminated this simple prayer in homilies addressed to the people of Ravenna, Italy.

Eventually — and quite naturally — Christians added in the names of the Savior and his mother. The angel's simple greeting "Hail" became "Hail Mary"; and Elizabeth's praise for "the fruit of your womb" was directed specifically to Jesus. The prayer underwent later development and, by the late Middle Ages, it seems to have reached the form we know today:

> Hail Mary, full of grace, the Lord is with thee; blessed art thou amongst women, and blessed is the fruit of thy womb, Jesus. Holy Mary, Mother of God, pray for us sinners, now and at the hour of our death. Amen.

The second half of the prayer includes common invocations of Mary that were already traditional in the Church as early as the third century. The phrase "Mother of God" was used by many Church Fathers and confirmed by the Council of Ephesus in A.D. 431.

The Hail Mary is the loving, confident prayer of people who know themselves to be brothers and sisters of Jesus Christ. With Jesus they call God "Father." With Jesus they call Mary "Mother."

The Glory Be. This prayer, sometimes called the Doxology, is modeled after the prayer the angels sang to announce the birth of Jesus to shepherds (Luke 2:14). The angels gave "glory to God in the highest." We name the triune God to whom we give glory: Father, Son, and Holy Spirit.

Doxology comes from the Greek words *doxa* (glory) and *logia* (saying). This prayer is simply a burst of glory or praise for almighty God — not for what he has done in history, but simply for who he is in essence, in eternity.

> Glory be to the Father, and to the Son, and to the Holy Spirit; as it was in the beginning, is now and ever shall be, world without end. Amen.

Sometimes we'll find the prayer in a slightly more modern form:

> Glory to the Father, and to the Son, and to the Holy Spirit; as it was in the beginning, is now, and will be forever. Amen.

The Glory Be shares a common ancestor with the Gloria we recite or sing at Mass on Sundays and holy days. Sometimes this short form is called the "Minor Doxology" to distinguish it from the longer version we use in the liturgy.

Praise is the purest and most perfect form of prayer because it is offered simply for God's sake. This little prayer — *Glory!* — has been, throughout history, the Christian's most common prayer of praise.

Life gives us many opportunities to say a short prayer, and these basic prayers serve that purpose very well. If we find out from an e-mail that a friend is suffering from an illness, we can say a Hail Mary. When we find that traffic is trying our patience, we can say an Our Father. When we're feeling great affection for our God — or when we feel that he's trying our patience — we can say a Glory Be. Like Erik Satie, we can begin every day with the Sign of the Cross.

When we use these prayers faithfully, they become habitual. We burn deep neural pathways that are hard to eradicate. The story of Erik Satie is hardly unique. Any parish priest will recognize it, at least in rough outline. How often we clergy are called to the hospital to visit a Catholic long out of touch with the faith, now facing the prospect of serious illness or death. They might not remember the name of the current pope. They might not be able to count off the Ten Commandments. But they can usually make the Sign of the Cross and join in the three basic prayers, once we get them started.

The basic prayers are simple, but they're rich. If we pray them mindfully, we are contemplating the Trinity of the Godhead and the fact that the eternal Word became flesh in Jesus Christ. We are acknowledging the fact that we are children of God in baptism. We are owning up to our own neediness — confessing that we can't do without our daily bread and we can't persevere to the hour of death unless we have God's grace.

Tradition has packed a lot into these little prayers. And each of them can serve as a prelude to the prayers that are welling up within your heart. As the author Bishop Robert Barron likes to say, "prayers lead to prayer." Formulas give form to our deepest longings.

You'll find the basic prayers packaged in many different combinations. Maybe your confessor will ask you to say an Our Father and two Hail Marys as your penance. If you visit some traditional pilgrimage routes, you may be instructed to say an Our Father at each station along the way. Many traditional novenas conclude with an Our Father, a Hail Mary, and a Glory Be.

The most popular configuration of the three basic prayers, however, is in the devotion we call the Rosary.

The Rosary is a form of meditation that engages many senses. If we pray aloud, it engages our hearing. If we pray before an image, it engages our sight. If we count our prayers on beads, it engages our touch. Most of all, in its "mysteries," it engages the mind in contemplation of certain scenes in the lives of Jesus and Mary. There are four sets of five mysteries.

> *The Joyful Mysteries*: 1. The Annunciation. 2. The Visitation. 3. The Birth of Jesus. 4. The Presentation in the Temple. 5. The Finding of the Child Jesus in the Temple.

> *The Luminous Mysteries*: 1. The Baptism of the Lord. 2. The Wedding Feast at Cana. 3. The Proclamation of the Kingdom. 4. The Transfiguration. 5. The Institution of the Eucharist at the Last Supper.

> *The Sorrowful Mysteries*: 1. The Agony in the Garden. 2. The Scourging at the Pillar. 3. The Crowning with Thorns. 4. The Carrying of the Cross. 5. The Crucifixion.

> *The Glorious Mysteries*: 1. The Resurrection. 2. The Ascension. 3. The Descent of the Holy Spirit at Pentecost. 4. The Assumption of Mary. 5. The Coronation of Mary.

The prayers of the Rosary are arranged in "decades" — one Our Father, followed by ten Hail Marys, concluding with a Glory Be. It is customary to pray five decades in sequence, and most Rosary beads are arranged that way. St. John Paul recommended that we pray the Joyful Mysteries on Monday and Saturday, the Luminous Mysteries on

Thursday, the Sorrowful Mysteries on Tuesday and Friday, and the Glorious Mysteries on Wednesday and Sunday.

The Rosary is part of the spiritual program of many — if not most — Catholics who follow a regular plan of prayer, no matter their level of income, education, or theological sophistication. The beads are beloved by people in remote Andean villages and by the most brilliant of theologians. It was a favorite prayer of Cardinal Avery Dulles, Blessed Mother Teresa of Calcutta, and Pope St. John Paul II. The movie director John Ford loved it and considered it to be his strongest argument for the faith. Once, when a reporter declared himself an atheist, Ford simply pressed his Rosary beads into the young man's hands. The football coach Knute Rockne died clutching his beads. Vietnam War hero Admiral Jeremiah Denton said that the Rosary kept him sane through long periods in solitary confinement. It was the prayer that Jacques Maritain said as he sat beside the deathbed of Erik Satie.

Dismissed by would-be reformers, the Rosary keeps coming back more popular than ever. Some years ago I recorded a series of meditations on the mysteries, and it sold so well in my hometown that the record stores put it on prominent display — emblazoned with a sticker that said "HOT!"

I didn't complain. The Rosary does keep the fires burning in our prayer.

CHAPTER 7

Morning Offering and Night Prayer

Academy Award winner Denzel Washington was asked to give advice to a group of young actors. He smiled and told them perhaps the last thing they would have expected. He said: "Put your shoes way under the bed at night so that you gotta get on your knees in the morning to find them. And while you're down there thank God for grace and mercy and understanding."[10]

That's good, practical advice, because it gets us into the posture of prayer and halfway into the act, at two times when forgetfulness is most common. We tend to be groggy when we're near the bed; and it's hard to formulate thoughts when we're sleepy, either with morning sluggishness or nighttime weariness. Yet it's extremely important that we *give* those moments to God, before they're *taken* by anything else.

If we strive to begin any task well and then end it well, most of the time we'll accomplish it well, even if some things go wrong along the way. The same is true of our days. Even if we seem to fail at so much that passes between 9 a.m. and 9 p.m., we usually have it in our power at least to begin well and end well. We can do this by starting and finishing every day with prayer.

We've all had the experience of waking up on the wrong side of the bed — hearing the alarm, feeling out of sorts, and dreading the start of the workday. Such feelings can lead to negative thoughts, and soon a bad day becomes a self-fulfilling prophecy.

Morning prayer stops that train of thought and sets it on a better track. If we simply make the effort to say our short prayers, we find ourselves on an elevated track. We're beginning to see the day from God's perspective. We're considering the near future according to divine categories rather than our own fears or feelings. Prayer doesn't make difficulties go away (usually), but it leaves us better equipped to deal with difficulties. We look ahead to any impending hardship with the sure knowledge that our Father God is with us at every moment.

Catholic tradition gives us many possible ways to begin our day. Two popular options are the Morning Offering and the Benedictus.

The Morning Offering is a simple prayer, but it manifests a rich theology. It differs from other forms of prayer, such as simple thanksgiving or contrition. It is an *offering* — an act of sacrifice — a priestly act.

"The whole Church is a priestly people," says the *Catechism of the Catholic Church* (CCC 1591; see also 1547, 1141, and 1268). "Through Baptism all the faithful share in the priesthood of Christ (CCC 1591)." Just as the Church's ordained priests offer the Body of Christ on the altar, so the laity consecrate the world to God. This participation is called the "common priesthood of the faithful."[11]

The Morning Offering is an explicit and all-inclusive act of consecration.

There are many different versions of the Morning Offering, but all of them express the same idea: that we give everything to God — everything that happens all day long, whether it seems good to us, or bad, or indifferent. Here is a version quite similar to the one that was widely taught in Catholic schools when I was a child.

> O Jesus, through the Immaculate Heart of Mary, I offer you all my prayers, works, joys, and sufferings of this day for all the intentions of your Sacred Heart, in union with the Holy Sacrifice of the Mass throughout the world, in reparation for my sins, for the intentions of all my relatives and friends, and in particular for the intentions of the Holy Father. Amen.

The Morning Offering makes sense out of the sufferings, both small and large, that we may undergo in the course of the day. We offer those sufferings as Jesus offered his, for the sake of others, and so our pain and hardship become redemptive. They become acts of love — for our relatives and friends, and even for the pope. We cultivate the kind of attitude St. Paul had. He could look ahead to hard times and say: "Now I rejoice in my sufferings for your sake, and in my flesh I complete what is lacking in Christ's afflictions for the sake of his body, that is, the Church" (Colossians 1:24). Suffering for love became, for him, a cause for joy. It wasn't pointless, senseless, or useless. His hardships had meaning, and so can ours, when we "offer them up." And that's what we do in our Morning Offering.

When we pray the Morning Offering, we give our day to God; we re-orient any negative thoughts; and we help to redeem and sanctify the world, beginning with those who are closest to us. Those are pretty impressive accomplishments, and they're already done by the time we reach the shoes under our bed.

The second common option for a morning prayer is the Benedictus. It is a longer prayer of praise for almighty God. It reviews the marvels God has done in the past; and it reminds us of his promises for the future. Thus it can help us begin our days on a note of hope and strength.

The Benedictus is found in its entirety in the Gospel of Luke (1:68–79). It is the prayer raised by the priest Zechariah when the elderly man recovers his speech at the birth of his son (St. John the Baptist).

For many centuries, priests and members of religious orders have prayed the Benedictus near the conclusion of the official Morning Prayer of the Church, in the Liturgy of the Hours. This is the most familiar form.

Benedictus (Canticle of Zechariah)

Blessed be the Lord, the God of Israel;
he has come to his people and set them free.

He has raised up for us a mighty savior,
born of the house of his servant David.

Through his holy prophets he promised of old
that he would save us from our enemies,
from the hands of all who hate us.

He promised to show mercy to our fathers
and to remember his holy covenant.

This was the oath he swore to our father Abraham:
to set us free from the hands of our enemies,
free to worship him without fear,

holy and righteous in his sight,
all the days of our life.

You, my child, shall be called the prophet of the
Most High;
For you will go before the Lord to prepare his way,
to give his people knowledge of salvation
by the forgiveness of their sins.

In the tender compassion of our God
the dawn from on high shall break upon us,
to shine on those who dwell in darkness and
the shadow of death,
and to guide our feet into the way of peace.
Amen.

Ending well is as important as beginning well; and so tradition also teaches us a certain way of approaching the end of the day.

As we prepare for sleep, we can take a moment to review our day in the presence of God. We will discuss this practice, the Examination of Conscience, in our chapter on Acts of Contrition.

Day's end is also a good time to thank God for specific blessings received during the day — answered prayers, temptations overcome, and other graces. A good act of thanksgiving is the opening line of Psalm 107: "O give thanks to the LORD, for he is good; for his mercy endures forever!"

The practice of gratitude is good for us. It helps us to focus on the positive aspects of life, which usually far outnumber our hardships. We tend to get used to good things, however, and take them for granted; and then a single downturn can make us feel overwhelmingly sad. An act of thanksgiving at the end of the day can renew us in joy, reminding us of all that God has given us.

Many Christians take this moment also to remember that their time on earth is finite. Death is our common end, but for believers that is not a morbid thought. Life is changed at death, not ended. If we have been faithful in life, it is changed for the better.

A customary night prayer is the Nunc Dimittis, yet another canticle from St. Luke's Gospel (2:29–32). It is the joyful song sung by the devout man Simeon as he encountered his long-awaited savior, the baby Jesus. Here is a traditional rendering of that prayer:

> Lord, now you let your servant go in peace;
> your word has been fulfilled:
> my own eyes have seen the salvation
> which you have prepared in the sight of every
> people:
> a light to reveal you to the nations
> and the glory of your people Israel.

In the Liturgy of the Hours, this canticle is followed by a Glory Be and then by the following brief but beautiful prayer: "Protect us, Lord, as we stay awake; watch over us as we sleep, that awake we may keep watch with Christ, and asleep rest in his peace."

If we make a habit of ending each day well, we're far more likely to end our life well. Each examination of conscience is a rehearsal for judgment, with its judgment and mercy. The joy of each thanksgiving anticipates a joy that we hope will be everlasting.

In the meantime, we should perhaps keep pushing our shoes "way under the bed."

CHAPTER 8

Devotion to Jesus in the Eucharist

Her husband's health was failing, but his doctors held out hope if he could move from New York to a more congenial climate. Elizabeth did not hesitate. She made plans to take William, along with the eldest of their five children, to live in Italy until William recovered.

They made the voyage by ship in 1803, and William's condition worsened at sea. He died soon after their ship docked in Italy. Elizabeth and her young daughter could not make an immediate return voyage, so they stayed with the family of William's business partner, Filippo Filicchi.

Elizabeth had had a privileged upbringing among the wealthy in her native land. Her social circle was entirely Protestant. The only Catholics she knew about in New York were poor. They were servants or criminals, the object of scorn or condescension.

Living with the Filicchis, however, she encountered a deep faith, unlike anything she had seen in her churchgoing life. The family was especially devoted to Jesus truly present in the Eucharist. They devoutly attended Mass, not only on Sundays, but whenever they could. Since Jesus' presence abides in the Sacrament, they would visit him in their church's tabernacle. They would march with him when, on feast days, he was carried through the streets in procession.

Elizabeth had been taught that Catholics worshipped idols; but she could see that the Filicchis worshipped Jesus, and that they did so more ardently than anyone she had ever met. Moreover, Elizabeth saw that this worship had a profound effect on the family's everyday life: as Jesus gave himself in the Eucharist, so the Filicchis gave themselves in charity and service to others. And the Filicchis were hardly unique. Their devotion was fairly typical of the people who lived in their city.

Yet her upbringing trumped this evidence. She resisted the attraction of Catholicism because the social cost of conversion would be too great. She would be ostracized. She could lose custody of her children.

One day a procession passed beneath her window, and she made the decision to watch secretly, but not to kneel as the Sacrament went by. As the parade approached, however, she felt compelled: "I fell on my knees … when the Blessed Sacrament passed by, and I cried to God to bless me … my whole soul desired only Him."[12]

It was a turning point. Elizabeth returned to New York and soon was received into full communion with the Catholic Church. She had known many joys in marriage and childrearing, but the day of her first Communion, she said, was the happiest day of her life.

She did not lose her children. She made history. Elizabeth Ann Seton opened the first Catholic school in the United States. She founded the country's first religious congregation for women. She fostered in others a deep devotion to Jesus in the Blessed Sacrament. She was the first native-born citizen of the United States to be canonized a saint.

From the first generation, the devotional life of Catholics has been intensely Eucharistic: "They held steadfastly to the apostles' teaching and fellowship, to the breaking of bread and to the prayers" (Acts 2:42). When Jesus established the Sacrament, he gave a command: "This is my body which is given for you," he said. "Do this in remembrance of me" (Luke 22:19). What's more, he made it clear that the Eucharist is not something optional in Christian life: "Truly, truly, I say to you, unless you eat the flesh of the Son of Man and drink his blood, you have no life in you" (John 6:53).

Jesus said, "Do this," so the Mass is what we do. The Mass gives us the life we have in us, just as it gave the Filicchi family a distinctive life that was abundantly evident to Elizabeth Seton.

The Eucharist is, according to the Second Vatican Council, the source and summit of Christian life. It is Jesus, and so it is the source of our life and love. Yet it is our goal as well — again, *because it is Jesus*. In the Eucharist, Jesus is truly and entirely present: body, blood, soul, and divinity. He is more present to us than he was to his Apostles during his public ministry, even though they could see his face and limbs and we cannot. We can receive him into our bodies and souls; they could not.

We need to place the Eucharist at the center of our prayer life, because that is how Jesus himself *designed* our prayer life. What does that mean, practically speaking? It means we will obey the law of the Church, which requires us to attend Mass on Sundays and certain holy days. That is a sweet requirement, more an opportunity than an obligation.

It means more than that, however. It means we will always feel a kind of gravitational tug toward Jesus' Real

Presence. We will exceed the letter of the law and find our way to the Sacrament more often than we are required. Like the family with whom St. Elizabeth Seton stayed, we will receive Jesus when we can and visit him.

Daily Mass is the ideal centerpiece for our program of prayer. The benefits of this practice are so numerous that they could themselves fill a book. (They have, in fact, filled many books.)

The Mass is the most God can do for us. He gives us his body, blood, soul, and divinity. God is almighty, infinite, and eternal, and yet he shares everything he has with you and me. Even God could not give us more than himself. If he made himself visible to us, that would be less. If he spoke audibly to us, that would still be less than he gives us in Holy Communion.

The Mass gives our spiritual life a needed dimension: community. Most of our devotional life is personal and private. The Mass, however, is necessarily communal. We gather with others from the parish, clergy and laity.

The Mass includes all the types of prayer. It is an act of adoration that includes contrition, thanksgiving, and supplication. It is the offering of Jesus himself, so it is the most complete prayer.

The Mass proclaims God's mighty deeds. At every Mass, the Church proclaims the Scriptures, both the Old Testament and the New Testament. Over the course of a three-year lectionary cycle, daily Massgoers will hear much of the contents of the Holy Bible. There is no more effective Bible-study program.

The Holy Spirit is active in the Mass — active in the preaching of the clergy and in our hearing of the word. If we attend attentively, we will be changed for the better.

In the Mass we are caught up in the current of the Church year. We celebrate the feasts and seasons of our faith. Every year we live through the cycle of Jesus' incarnation and growth, passion and death, resurrection and glorification.

Many people find that weekday Mass is a more intimate experience than Sunday Mass. The crowd is smaller. The Church is quieter and more conducive to prayer. The people are there because they want to be there, not because they feel obliged. There is a quiet intensity to the participation. It is right for us to go on Sundays, when everyone is there. But it is better for us to go more often, and even daily, if our schedule allows.

Jesus' presence in the Eucharist is abiding. That means he remains present even after the Mass is ended. Our churches reserve the Sacrament in their tabernacles, and we mark his presence with a sanctuary lamp.

When I was a child, it was customary for Catholics to make the Sign of the Cross when they passed a Catholic Church. They did this as an act of faith. They knew Jesus was there. Men would tip their hats as they drove by.

And many would not go by without dropping in. Fr. Ronald Lawler, the Capuchin priest who was for many years my spiritual director, once said of his mother: "She did not walk past churches. Churches were for going into."[13] Shopping bags in hand, she took her young son inside to visit Jesus in the tabernacle. That was, Fr. Lawler recalled, how he acquired "ordinary faith in the Eucharist."

It's a good practice to take up: making visits to the Blessed Sacrament. If there is a church on our way to or from work, this can be done fairly easily, and it won't require much time.

Even if the Church is locked, we can still benefit from Jesus' nearness. We are making an act of faith. We are acknowledging the effort he has made to remain with us.

A priest friend of mine lived for many years at a suburban parish near Pittsburgh. The church was on a major thoroughfare, but at night the property was quiet and dark. He began to notice, however, that a car pulled into the parking lot at the same time every night. The driver would park beside the church, idle there for a minute, and then drive off.

This went on for several nights, and Father began to worry. Was the parish property being used for drug deals? He decided to confront the driver next time the car appeared.

The next night he was waiting with his shoes on, and he walked briskly to the lot when he saw the car pull in. He was surprised, however, to see a familiar face in the driver's seat — a young mother of several small children, who was very active in the parish.

"Hi, Father!" she said. "You're probably wondering what I'm doing." She went on to explain that she needed to be with Jesus, and the only opportune moment was after the last child went to bed. She "visited" from the spot in the parking lot that was nearest to the church's tabernacle.

Experts in prayer have made the same discovery. Thomas Merton was a Trappist monk and bestselling author of books on spirituality. He wanted to go deeper in prayer, so he asked permission to live alone in a hermitage. His superiors gave the okay, and Fr. Merton went off into the woods. But after a couple years of this life he came to the conclusion that he wasn't making progress. Why? He didn't have Jesus' abiding presence with him. So he went back to his superiors and asked their permission to keep a tabernacle in the hermitage. They granted permission; and he said it made a vast difference in the intensity of his prayer.

If we can spend even a little time with Jesus this way, where he is truly present, it will have an outsized effect over time.

Daily Mass is an investment of time, but the dividends are as immense as we sincerely wish them to be. Many busy people know this, and so they make time for Mass or a visit to Jesus — or both. I have been a bishop for many years, and so I have offered thousands of weekday Masses in cathedrals and other city parishes. There, every day, I saw the same faces: the crew that cleaned the office buildings, who stopped in at church at the end of the night shift; the bank and advertising executives, who went to Mass before their workdays began; the young parents with their children in tow; the students who sought wisdom for their studies and strength for their exams. James Joyce called the crowd at Mass "Here Comes Everybody," and so it is.

That's Jesus' design for parish life — and for the spiritual life of each of us individually.

CHAPTER 9

Acts of Contrition

"Blessed are the pure in heart," Jesus said, "for they shall see God" (Matthew 5:8). And our experience bears this out. When we strive for simplicity and integrity — when our intentions are pure and our actions are true — we draw closer to the Lord. Our thoughts match our words, and our words match our deeds, and so we can approach our heavenly Father unimpeded by guilt or shame.

People since Adam and Eve have, however, maintained such integrity only with difficulty — with divine grace matched by the grit of human effort. St. Paul observed that "all have sinned and fall short of the glory of God" (Romans 3:23); and few people have bothered to argue against that assertion.

St. Paul did not see the universality of sin as a reason to despair. For the Gospel he preached, the Good News of Jesus Christ, was "redemption, the forgiveness of sins" (Colossians 1:14). God will forgive our sins when we express our sorrow, even though we fall repeatedly. Paul was raised from childhood with the adage: "a righteous man falls seven times, and rises again; but the wicked are overthrown by calamity" (Proverbs 24:16).

Sin frustrates us; but our tradition gives us many strategies for avoiding and repenting of sin, and these methods of prayer should be an important part of our plan of life.

We call our expressions of repentance, collectively, "acts of contrition."

Contrition means sorrow for sin, joined with a true purpose of amendment — our intention to avoid this or that particular sin in the future. Sometimes we're moved to feel sorry out of true hatred for our sins and pure love for God; such a movement of the heart is called *perfect contrition*. Other times we are motivated, perhaps, by fear of the consequences of our sins; we fear punishment. This is called *imperfect contrition*. Both love and fear are helpful motives, though love is certainly the better of the two.

An act is a deed. When we *act*, we do something. Something gets done. So with an Act of Contrition, we pray a prayer. The prayer can take many forms. If we simply say, "Lord, I'm sorry," we have made an Act of Contrition.

An ancient prayer of repentance, popular in the Eastern churches, is called the Jesus Prayer: "Lord Jesus Christ, Son of God, have mercy on me, a sinner."

A fuller Act of Contrition is the one that has been taught to children for the last few generations. I say it's fuller because it expresses not just sorrow for sins, but also the desire to change one's life. It acknowledges God's grace, but it also promises that the grace will not be wasted — that we will correspond to any heavenly help with our earthly effort.

> O my God, I am heartily sorry for having offended you, and I detest all my sins, because I dread the loss of heaven and the pains of hell, but most of all because they offend you, my God, who are all-good and deserving of all my love. I firmly resolve, with the help of your

> grace, to confess my sins, to do penance, and to amend my life. Amen.

It begins with sorrow but ends with resolution. It's a prayer that begins in the depths, but ends with a lot of upward and forward momentum. The Act of Contrition is an effective means of progress in the spiritual life. Remember: sin is what sullies the heart and keeps it from "seeing" God. Contrition is prayer that purifies us and makes greater prayer possible.

We should make some brief Act of Contrition — even just the words "Lord, have mercy" — whenever we become aware that we have sinned. We need not make our Act of Contrition aloud. It should arise from our heart, but it can remain a silent prayer of the heart.

We can offer an Act of Contrition whenever the need comes up; but we should have at least one time every day when we do it. We should use it to end our daily *examination of conscience.*

The examination of conscience is an ancient Christian custom. It's the moment we take to review our day, trying to see it as God saw it. If your days are busy, it can be helpful to look over your appointment book and ask God to help you to judge your moral performance. We can thank God for the gifts and special graces that enabled us to do good. We should also express sorrow for any choices we've made that are contrary to God's law or the good of others. This is the moment when we can candidly admit to God any moral failure in our thoughts, words, actions, or omissions. We don't need to scrutinize too closely. We don't need to be overly scrupulous. Our examination of conscience should take three to five minutes.

Most people make their examination at night, shortly before going to bed. Pope St. John XXIII recommended making a very brief exam also at midday — so that, if we notice things are going badly, we can correct our course for the rest of the day. It seems to have worked well for him. Though he spent much of his adult life in very high-pressure jobs, people remember him for his patience and his cheer.

Some spiritual writers recommend dividing the examination of conscience into two parts, a general examination and a particular examination. What we have already described is the general part. A particular examination would focus on our efforts in a specific area of life — whether we're making progress in acquiring a certain virtue or rooting out a certain vice. We can concentrate on courage, for example, or kindness, or industry. Or we can struggle to overcome eating between meals, negative speech, or other habits our coworkers or family members find annoying. A particular examination can be changed regularly. As we make progress in one area of life, we can shift our attention to another. Over the course of a year — and a lifetime — this practice can help us to see the practical difference our habits of prayer are making.

St. Paul knew the value of this practice. He advised the Corinthian Christians: "Examine yourselves, to see whether you are holding to your faith. Test yourselves. Do you not realize that Jesus Christ is in you?" (2 Corinthians 13:5; see also 1 Corinthians 11:28).

Since Jesus Christ is in us, we should behave accordingly. Are we living each hour, each day, as we should? At our daily examination of conscience, we can make that judgment call with God's help.

The examination of conscience should lead us to a healthy self-knowledge. I emphasize that such self-knowledge, for a Catholic, is healthy. It's good for us to recognize our own weaknesses, foibles, and *faux pas*. It's better, though, that we can do something with that knowledge. We can set ourselves a program for overcoming particular sins — and we can seek definitive forgiveness of the sins we've committed, the sins we've discovered through our examination of conscience.

We can be sure of the forgiveness we receive in the Sacrament of Confession (also known as Reconciliation or Penance).

Sins are different than crimes. Crimes are offenses against the civic order, so civil authorities can "forgive" crimes and waive punishments. But sins are offenses against God, and "God alone" has the power to forgive sins (see Mark 2:7). Yet this is one of the powers he has shared with the Church.

On the day he rose from the dead, Jesus appeared to his Apostles and said to them: "Peace be with you. As the Father has sent me, even so I send you.... Receive the Holy Spirit. If you forgive the sins of any, they are forgiven; if you retain the sins of any, they are retained" (John 20:21–23). So important was this privilege that the first clergy understood their mission to be a "ministry of reconciliation" (2 Corinthians 5:18). Sacramental forgiveness was a key element of the Church's life throughout its early history. It remains so today.

For that we can give thanks. When we make an examination of conscience, we confront the parts of our lives and the corners of our personality that are least pleasant to see. No one enjoys admitting their faults. We'd much rather cover up, save face, and shift blame elsewhere. But that's not right, and we know it.

The better thing to do is to go to Confession. The self-knowledge we gain by examining our days need not — and should not — lead us to a dead end of regret and remorse. Jesus established the Sacrament of Confession so that God himself can repair the damage we've done to our relationship with him. He wants only our movement of sorrow, our expression of contrition, spoken aloud to God in the person of his priest. There, God does for our sins what earthly judges can do for our crimes. He forgives us — and yet he does so much more. Because he has divine power, he also gives us the grace to avoid the sin in the future. If we keep going back to the sacrament, he will give us the strength we need to overcome the sin altogether. It may take many years; but God is patient, and he wants us to grow more Godlike as we learn patience, too.

It is impossible to overstate the importance of regular sacramental Confession for anyone who is serious about cultivating a spiritual life. The popes of the last forty years have all admitted to going to Confession at least once a week. That's admirable. We should strive to go at least once a month.

We should set that day and have it on our calendar. We can target the regular Confession time at our parish, or trek to a parish where nobody knows us, or make an appointment at a nearby monastery. It doesn't matter. We just need to make the commitment — set the date and time — and follow through, again and again.

Some time ago I wrote a book on Confession, and I'm resisting the temptation now to reproduce that book in this chapter.[14] Confession is that important.

Sometimes it's also urgent. The late Fr. Bertin Roll, a Capuchin priest in my hometown of Pittsburgh, had a long-standing reputation as an excellent confessor. You would never hear him (or any priest) talk about what he'd heard in the confessional. Priests are bound to observe the "seal of the confessional," which is absolute. But Fr. Bertin shared many amusing stories about the *circumstances* in which he'd heard confessions.

Once he was walking down the front steps of an inner-city church when a taxi screeched to a halt in front of him. A man jumped out of the back seat and shouted, "Hey, Father, can you hear my confession?" Fr. Bertin nodded yes, to the man's great excitement. The man told the cabbie to wait and rushed to Fr. Bertin's side. Before beginning to confess his sins, he urged the priest to be quick with his forgiveness. "Remember, Father, the meter on that cab is running!"

Another time Fr. Bertin was sitting in city traffic, and he came to an intersection where a policeman was directing cars through the gridlock. The officer saw Fr. Bertin's Roman collar and asked, through the car's open window, if he had time to hear a Confession. Fr. Bertin agreed, and the officer jumped into the front seat and started confessing. The gridlock could wait till absolution.

These are, of course, extraordinary cases. If we recognize Confession's importance and make time for it regularly, we can keep our souls from needing it so urgently!

If sin will be part of life as long as we're on earth — and it seems that it will be — then Acts of Contrition, examinations of conscience, and Confession should be an essential part of our plan. They work together for our good, to purify our hearts so that we can "see God," first in our prayer and then in heaven.

CHAPTER 10

Spiritual Reading

Iñigo de Loyola was a proud young man — and he had reason to be proud. He had served valiantly in battle, defending the Spanish city of Pamplona with just a handful of men against an advancing French army of twelve thousand. The French laid siege to the city; and, in the artillery barrage that followed, a cannonball struck Iñigo, passing through his legs, breaking his right shin and tearing open his left calf.

He had been prepared to die in battle, but not to be severely wounded. His torn leg raged with infection. His broken leg had to be set, and then broken again, and then reset. It would be a long convalescence, seemingly endless to an adventurer like Iñigo. All he could do, really, was read — and what thrill was there in reading?

He asked his caretakers to bring him books about knights and battles — the swashbuckling romances of King Arthur and Amadis of Gaul. He would live through the exploits of these literary heroes. But no such books could be found. All his caretakers could round up were a life of Jesus Christ and some biographies of the saints.

Iñigo felt his choice was stark. He could read the books he had at hand, or he could die of boredom. So he picked up a book, and then another, and then another.

From Jesus and from the saints, the young warrior learned about a different sort of adventure. He came to see the heroism in holiness. In these books, all the warfare was spiritual; but Iñigo saw that the stakes were much higher, the risks much greater, the deeds more daring. Soon he aspired to rival the great saints in the practice of fasting, vigils, and pilgrimage — just as he had once longed to outdo Sir Lancelot on the field of battle.

Books brought Iñigo to a new life, and it would indeed be a life of adventure. Now he would gather a band about him and make conquests for the glory of a great king, Jesus Christ. Iñigo, known to posterity as St. Ignatius of Loyola, founded the Society of Jesus, commonly called the Jesuits, one of the mightiest religious organizations in the history of the world. St. Ignatius' own books, especially his *Spiritual Exercises*, are now, more than four hundred years after his death, considered classics of the genre.

His truly great life began with good spiritual reading — and he has brought a better life to many others *through reading!*

The life of Ignatius is hardly unique in this respect. Many great figures have traced the turning point in their lives to their reading of a passage from a book.

In the fourth century, young Augustine heard a neighborhood child sing, "Take up and read, take up and read," and he reached for the nearest book at hand. In St. Paul's Letter to the Romans, he recounts the passage that inspired him to give up his sinful habits.

In the twentieth century, a young student at Columbia University, Thomas Merton, took down at random a book from a library shelf. It was *The Spirit of Medieval Philosophy*, by Etienne Gilson, and it set him on the road to Catholic faith. Other recent converts followed similar paths, through the chapters of good spiritual books. The social activist Dorothy Day, for example, read St. Thérèse of Lisieux's *Story of a Soul* and it transformed her. The novelist Walker Percy, a high-flying intellectual, was converted by a very simple book, *Father Smith Instructs Jackson*, by Bishop John Noll.

My own life took a turn for the better when I was twelve years old and a parish priest, Fr. Joseph Bryan, suggested I read *Introduction to the Devout Life*, by St. Francis de Sales. I am still meditating on that book, more than sixty years later, and still using the same copy.

Spiritual reading is part of the daily regimen of most serious Christians. It's a discipline, like any kind of reading; yet it differs from other reading in important ways. It's not simply "study"; it's not research. It's not just fact-gathering and "book learning."

Spiritual reading is our *prayerful* consideration of a religious text that merits such attention. Spiritual reading is a form of prayer as much as it is an exercise in reading. We should go about it in a deliberate and meditative way, savoring the words in God's presence. It's good to read slowly.

It's best to begin our reading with a prayer, acknowledging God's presence and calling for help. The traditional prayer to the Holy Spirit suits this occasion well:

> Come, Holy Spirit, fill the hearts of your faithful and kindle in them the fire of your love. Send forth your Spirit and they shall be created. And you shall renew the face of the earth.
>
> O God, you instructed the hearts of the faithful by the light of the Holy Spirit. Grant that by the same Holy Spirit we may be truly

> wise and ever enjoy his consolations, through Christ Our Lord. Amen.

A shorter form of the prayer is the simple aspiration "Come, Holy Spirit!" — and that will suffice.

And then we read.

What do we read in spiritual reading? We should choose a book that is worthy of our prayerful reflection. It could be a book about prayer, or morals, or dogma, or the nature of God. It could be a biography, a long poem, a sermon, or letters of counsel. The treasury of spiritual literature is rich.

It may be a book by an author whom the Church has canonized or beatified — a saint or a blessed. The most helpful authors are those the popes have declared to be Doctors of the Church. The word doctor, as it's used here, carries its original Latin sense; it means teacher. There are more than thirty Doctors of the Church, and they should serve as our instructors in the ways of the spirit. The Doctors are saints whose works have formed many other saints.

It's good to get guidance in our reading, because not every great book is suitable for every person and every stage of the spiritual journey. St. Paul told the Corinthians that, when he preached to them, he gave them milk before solid food (see 1 Corinthians 3:2). We, too, need to work through much basic doctrine on our way to a purer contemplation of God. If we know a priest or layperson who is well read and spiritually mature, we might ask for recommendations of books to read.

We need not read a lot. It is better to read a little each day, but read deeply. Put aside ten or fifteen minutes for the task. It can be done while you're sipping your morning coffee or riding the subway home. The time and place should be suitable for concentration.

We can read on paper, on a smart phone, on a laptop, or using whatever medium we prefer. Many of the classics of spiritual literature are available free online in digital formats. Those are old translations, and not always as smooth to the ear as modern editions; but they serve the purpose if money is tight.

And we need not be deterred by eye fatigue, dyslexia, or even blindness. There is at least one website (MariaLectrix.WordPress.com) that makes available the classics of spiritual literature in audio-book formats, free of charge.

Books written in our own day are also suitable for spiritual reading. In fact, they can be especially helpful because they're written in familiar language, directly addressing today's concerns. In our own reading, we can, perhaps, alternate contemporary books with titles from the great tradition.

The most important book for spiritual reading is the Bible. It is, in fact, in a class by itself. Only the Bible gives us God's word in human words. No other book can be attributed to God as author who, through the Holy Spirit, "inspired the human authors of the sacred books" (CCC 105–106; see also 2 Timothy 3:16).

The Church applies a special term to the prayerful reading of Scripture. The practice is known as *lectio divina*, "divine reading." Lectio, according to Pope Francis, "consists of reading God's word in a moment of prayer and allowing it to enlighten and renew us."[15] Again, it is not like studying for an examination. It is, in fact, a dialogue with

God — who inspired the text and authored it, knowing that you and I would encounter it in a particular moment of prayer. The Bible itself tells us: "The word of God is living and active, sharper than any two-edged sword, piercing to the division of soul and spirit, of joints and marrow, and discerning the thoughts and intentions of the heart" (Hebrews 4:12). God knows how to reach into us through his inspired word.

Pope Benedict XVI described lectio as "poring over a biblical text for some time, reading it and rereading it … 'ruminating' on it as the Fathers say and squeezing from it, so to speak, all its 'juice,' so that it may nourish meditation and contemplation."[16]

Pope Francis gave us a sketch of how such a session might go forward.

> In the presence of God, during a recollected reading of the text, it is good to ask, for example: "Lord, what does this text say *to me*? What is it about my life that you want to change by this text? What troubles me about this text? Why am I not interested in this? Or perhaps: What do I find pleasant in this text? What is it about this word that moves me? What attracts me? Why does it attract me?
>
> When we make an effort to listen to the Lord, temptations usually arise. One of them is simply to feel troubled or burdened, and to turn away. Another common temptation is to think about what the text means for other people, and so avoid applying it to our own life. It can also happen that we look for excuses to water down the clear meaning of the text. Or

> we can wonder if God is demanding too much of us, asking for a decision which we are not yet prepared to make. This leads many people to stop taking pleasure in the encounter with God's word; but this would mean forgetting that no one is more patient than God our Father, that no one is more understanding and willing to wait. He always invites us to take a step forward, but does not demand a full response if we are not yet ready. He simply asks that we sincerely look at our life and present ourselves honestly before him, and that we be willing to continue to grow, asking from him what we ourselves cannot as yet achieve.[17]

We should not try to consume page after page in our time of prayerful Bible reading — or even many paragraphs. For our souls, Scripture is the strongest medicine, the richest food, and the purest fragrance. A small quantity will go a long way.

Pope Benedict held that lectio divina was the key to renewal, not only for individuals, but for the whole Church: "If it is effectively promoted, this practice will bring to the Church — I am convinced of it — a new spiritual springtime."[18]

God has revealed himself to you in Sacred Scripture. When you make a commitment to read the Bible daily, you are showing your appreciation and saying "thank you."

There are many ways to do this. You can read along with the Church using the cycle of readings used at daily Mass. The United States Conference of Catholic Bishops posts the daily readings on its website (USCCB.org). The site offers not only the readings of the day, but short video reflections that may help your own meditation and prayer. You can, if you wish, take in as much of the readings as will fill your pre-determined time. If you want to follow the lectionary, but prefer turning pages made of paper, you can use a missal or subscribe to a magazine (like *Magnificat*) that publishes the liturgical readings for each day of a given month.

But there are other ways of reading Scripture. You might decide to read a particular book from beginning to end. It's best to start with one of the Gospels and read just a little bit each day. This practice helps you enter into the mind of the human author, see the dramatic development of Jesus' life from his perspective, and gain a deeper appreciation of his unique concerns.

Again, the reading is only spiritual if it is prayerful. We should begin with prayer, and close with prayer, too, even if our closing prayer is simply the Sign of the Cross.

Spiritual reading shouldn't be a burden. It should be a joy, and sometimes even entertaining. After all, we're reading the authors whose works have endured for ages.

We can take our ten or fifteen minutes and divide them in whatever way we find helpful. We can allot half for Scripture and half for some other spiritual book. Or we can give more time to Scripture, since it's God's Word and demands more attention. Or we can give *less* time to Scripture because it's God's Word and its dosage is so much stronger!

There is no universal formula for spiritual reading. Its practice will vary with each believer. There is, however, overwhelming evidence that it works — that God has made many saints through good books.

CHAPTER 11

Mental Prayer

When Walter Ciszek volunteered to work as an undercover missionary in Russia, he knew the dangers he would face. The Soviet Union was officially atheist and the godless government controlled all religious activity. Religious believers were persecuted, and Catholics were especially suspect because they pledged loyalty to a "foreign power," the pope in Rome.

In formation as a Jesuit, Walter Ciszek accepted the risks and underwent special training as he prepared for ordination. He learned the languages of Eastern Europe. He learned the rites of the Eastern and Western churches. After he was ordained, he served at a parish in Poland; and in 1939 he found a way to enter Ukraine undetected. There he worked as a logger, practicing his ministry clandestinely.

In 1941 he was caught by the secret police and accused of spying for the Vatican. He expected to be tortured, but he thought he was tough enough to withstand it. He had, after all, undertaken rigorous penances during his Jesuit formation, and he had lived a demanding life.

He was not prepared, however, for the effects of solitary confinement. The Soviets jailed Fr. Ciszek in a windowless cell, where he had no human contact and no way to measure the passage of time — no sense of night or day, no sound of human voices.

He began to lose his vaunted self-discipline. Then he began to fear he was losing his mind. The Book of Genesis says: “It is not good that the man should be alone” (Genesis 2:18), and solitary confinement proves the point. Medical studies show that, after two days of isolation, a prisoner’s brain activity will shift toward stupor or delirium. Two weeks can cause permanent psychological damage.

Fr. Ciszek was walled up in Russia’s notorious Lubyanka prison for the greater part of five years.

What saved him was his decision to return to the “daily order,” the plan of life, that he had known in Jesuit formation. As soon as his jailers woke him, he would recite a morning offering. He would then pray the prayers of the Mass from memory, even though he had no bread or wine. He said the Angelus prayers three times a day. He sang hymns. He prayed three Rosaries — one in Latin, one in Polish, and one in Russian. He examined his conscience twice a day. But the largest block of time in his program was dedicated to mental prayer. Fr. Ciszek tried to dedicate a solid hour to meditative, conversational prayer each day.

His days — once a formless, endless stretch of apprehension and fear — began to assume a distinctive shape. Most importantly, Fr. Ciszek began to remember that he was not alone — that he could never be alone, even in solitary confinement, as long as he knew God’s nearness.

What is mental prayer — that it could work with such power in someone’s life?

The *Catechism of the Catholic Church* gives us the definition set down centuries ago by St. Teresa of Ávila. Mental prayer “is nothing else than a close sharing between friends;

it means taking time frequently to be alone with him who we know loves us."[19]

Mental prayer is our silent conversation with God. Prayer is "mental" when we express our thoughts and affections before God in our own terms, and not those of a pre-determined formula.

The terminology for this type of prayer is pretty fluid. Some people call it contemplative prayer, and others call it meditation. Still others call it interior prayer. You can use whichever term you prefer, but the important thing is to take up the practice.

We need to talk with God — not just talk *at* God, or talk *about* God. We need to practice the art of "close sharing" with the Father, Son, and Holy Spirit.

There is no other way to have a personal relationship. Love grows from company and conversation. That's true of friendship, marriage, and the sibling bond. We thrive on the time we spend together. God made us that way for a reason — so that we could learn to converse with him, too.

So we need to set time aside each day to spend in God's company, to speak and to listen. It is good for us, as it was good for Fr. Ciszek, to schedule time for particular devotions throughout the day — the Rosary, the Angelus, and so on — and these will surely engage our mind. Nevertheless, we should have a solid block of time when we give our attention entirely to the divine conversation.

How should we proceed?

It's best to find a quiet place, or at least a place conducive to concentration. The optimum place is in a church, where Jesus is present in the Blessed Sacrament. But it might be difficult to find a church unlocked at a time convenient for your schedule.

A room at home will do just fine. We should take a minute, however, to shut off the television, radio, or other noisemaker. It's good to silence our phones as well and close the laptop. In shoring up our silence, we're making a firm commitment to the Lord. We're going to give him the time we've promised. We're not keeping our options open, in case something more interesting comes along.

Though mental prayer is prayer free of formulas, it's good to begin with the most standard of formulas, the Sign of the Cross. Then we should acknowledge the Lord's presence and begin to speak to him about anything at all. If we find the process awkward, we can make that very awkwardness the subject of our prayer.

The topic of our conversation should be the stuff of our lives. We can talk to God about difficulties at work — or triumphs at work. We should talk to God about our relationships — with friends and family members, each individually considered. We should bring up the things that really concern us.

We should talk with God about heaven. We should talk with God about the divine nature, asking for light and understanding.

We can spend part of our time in mental prayer addressing the Blessed Mother and the saints, too — or the angels, especially our guardian angel.

Some people keep a notebook of topics they wish to bring up during their prayer, and they jot reminders in it throughout the day. Some people keep a list of words they would like to pray about — *love*, *communion*, *praise*, *grace* — and then turn these over in God's presence. We can also pray about a line of Scripture, using what we've learned from the practice of *lectio divina*.

In our prayer, however, we should make sure that our considerations do not veer into planning. When we're talking to God about work, for example, it can be easy for us simply to start working — mentally drafting the next memo or reviewing tomorrow's schedule. When we find that's happened, we should turn our thoughts back to God.

As we're talking to God about our worries, it can be easy for us to forget God and just let our worries run riot. When we find we've done that, we should give our worries over to God.

Now and then, we should stop talking and simply listen. This requires patience, because hearing God is not like hearing the people with whom we live and work. The soul does not have sensory organs. There is no instrument to record what the soul receives from God, and no gauge to measure the soul's response. So we may not recognize God's answers to us till days, months, or even years after they have had their effect.

Nor are our feelings a reliable indicator. We may experience favors and consolations that are gifts from God; yet they are not necessarily manifestations of our greatest spiritual growth. Our true progress may come with our dogged fidelity in prayer when we really don't feel like praying.

It's helpful to have a fixed time dedicated to the task. Many spiritual writers recommend a "holy hour," a full sixty minutes set aside for mental prayer; and that is ideal. But an hour may seem too long when we're just taking our first steps in prayer. Indeed, an hour may be more than a busy person can spare.

It's fine to start with a smaller increment, but we should strive to make it no less than twenty minutes. We need at least that much time in order to withdraw from the noise of our day and give ourselves over to the task of prayer.

We should try not to cut our time short, especially if we're finding it dry or unrewarding; and we should try not to linger in our mental prayer, even if we're finding it especially interesting. Sometimes we'll experience long stretches when the exercise seems pointless and God seems absent or silent. Other times we'll experience unusual joys. Our dedication should not depend upon these feelings. Our feelings are not the point. Our faithfulness is the point.

Inhibitions can hold back the progress of any relationship, and this is certainly true of our dealings with God. Sometimes people feel they should hide their true feelings from God, for fear of offending him. But God knows our hidden thoughts even better than we do. He knows our angers and our dissatisfactions. He knows well if we are angry or dissatisfied with the plan he has for us!

So it makes no sense for us to be inhibited. We can tell God how we feel, and tell him that we don't like feeling at odds with him, and then ask his grace to get over ourselves. That could be a most satisfactory moment of prayer, even though it began with frustration.

It might take time for us to relax into the habit of prayer. Long silences can be awkward in a conversation between two people who just met; but old friends and long-married couples can enjoy one another's company without multiplying words to fill every pause.

Our relationship with God can get to the same place; and that is a foretaste of heaven.

This chapter began with a long episode from the life of Fr. Walter Ciszek. I would be remiss if I left it unfinished.

Fr. Ciszek came to know that he was never alone. He emerged from years of solitary confinement as a psychologically healthy man. Why? Because he was never truly isolated. He spent more quality time in conversation each day than his jailers did; and his conversation was with the God who created him, redeemed him, and wanted to sanctify him. His conversation was with his heavenly Father, his divine Brother, and the Life of his soul.

Sentenced to years of hard labor in the coldest and most remote regions of Russia, Fr. Ciszek continued to exercise his priestly ministry, hearing Confessions and offering Mass while he worked as a miner, a mechanic, a builder, and a loader of barges. In 1963, after almost a quarter-century in custody, he was released and allowed to return to his native country.

Coming home to the United States, he spent his remaining two decades as a spiritual director, guiding people in the ways of mental prayer — the ways he had discovered for himself in solitude with God in Lubyanka prison.

Perhaps he gave the same advice his Jesuit brother, Pope Francis, would one day give the faithful: *Just close your eyes and talk to Jesus.*

CHAPTER 12

Fasting and Self-Denial

Orestes Brownson was raised, at the beginning of the nineteenth century, in a traditional New England farming family. His parents were Calvinist in doctrine and Congregationalist in their church affiliation. Orestes was a devout and exceptionally intelligent young man. In his youth, he began to question some doctrines of the Protestant Reformation. His investigations led him to abandon mainstream Christianity and to associate with Transcendentalists such as Henry David Thoreau and Ralph Waldo Emerson. Rejecting the Christian dogma of the Trinity, Brownson served as a clergyman for a while in Unitarian and Universalist congregations. He read widely in contemporary philosophy and the religions of the Far East. He founded an influential quarterly journal of literature, politics, and culture.

Still, he was not satisfied. His explorations and his experiences, in fact, led him back to some distinctively Christian notions — like sin, the need for redemption, and the need for a redeemer who was divine. As he studied history, he concluded that Jesus was indeed the divine redeemer, and that the Lord had established the Catholic Church as the ordinary means of salvation. With his wife and children, Orestes Brownson entered the Catholic Church in 1844, when he was forty-one years old.

He became zealous for Catholic practices, especially those of the ancient Church. He embraced the long-established customs of fasting and abstinence, and he refused to keep quiet about his newfound enthusiasm.

Shortly after his conversion, in the midst of travels, he found himself lodging at an inn in northern Massachusetts. It was Friday night, and the innkeeper set before his guests a sumptuous beef stew. Most of those at table were hungry men, and they responded with eagerness. But not Brownson.

"Have you *nothing*," he roared, "that a *Christian* can eat?"

The innkeeper didn't get his drift and replied that there was food enough for everyone.

Brownson went on to explain: "But today, sir, is Friday, and Christians do not eat meat on Friday!"[20]

At the time Orestes Brownson had his outburst, it was the law of the Church that all Catholics should observe meatless Fridays. As Brownson knew, the "Friday abstinence" was a custom kept since the generation of the Apostles.

To fast is to do without food for a specified period of time, or to do with less. To abstain is to do without a particular food or drink. In the earliest Christian documents we learn (as Brownson did) that first- and second-century believers fasted every Wednesday and every Friday. They fasted for longer stretches in preparation for Easter and at other times.

Why did the early Christians fast? Well, the most compelling reason was surely the model they found in the life of Jesus. "He fasted forty days and forty nights" (Matthew 4:2); and he assumed that his disciples would follow his example.

> And *when you fast*, do not look dismal, like the hypocrites, for they disfigure their faces that their fasting may be seen by men. Truly, I say to you, they have their reward. But *when you fast*, anoint your head and wash your face, that your fasting may not be seen by men but by your Father who is in secret; and your Father who sees in secret will reward you (Matthew 6:16–18, emphasis added).

Fasting is a devotion as old as the Old Testament, where it's taken up by prophets and kings. But, as Jesus made clear, fasting and self-denial are an important part of the Gospel as well, and they are an essential habit of any soul who would draw close to Christ and imitate him.

Fasting means many things in the Bible. It is a way to grow in humility (see Isaiah 58:5) and acknowledge one's sins (Jonah 3:5). It is an offering of intercession, a prayer for the good of another (Psalm 35:13). It is a form of worship (Luke 2:37).

Always, however, it is an expression of hope and expectation. To fast is to prepare oneself for some great event. Moses fasted in the days before he received the Law from God (Deuteronomy 9:9). Elijah fasted before he received the word of the Lord (1 Kings 19:8). The prophetess Anna fasted in advance of the day she saw the Messiah (Luke 2:37). The Apostles fasted when they were about to make an important appointment (Acts 14:23).

Jesus, of course, hallowed the practice by his forty-day fast in the wilderness, on the eve of his public ministry. For him, fasting was not penitential, as it is for us, since he was sinless. He could only offer penitence on our behalf. And he was certainly preparing for something momentous.

Too often, Christians miss the positive meaning of fasting and self-denial. Yes, we give something up — but we do this because we are expecting something better. At a family meal we might forego a second helping of the main course, so that we "save room" for dessert. When we fast, we are "saving room" for God. We are telling the Lord that we prize him more than any material goods, even necessities such as food.

We do this with the expectation that God will fill us with himself. We know he will not let us down. We know this from the lives of Moses, Elijah, David, and Anna.

As Catholics, we have certain periods of fasting built into our devotional lives. We always fast from food or drink for one hour before receiving Holy Communion. On Ash Wednesday and Good Friday we take only one full meal and abstain from meat. On all the Fridays of Lent we abstain from meat. Throughout the season of Lent, it's traditional to "give up" something we ordinarily enjoy — to fast from sweets, for example, or social media.

It is customary also to observe some act of self-denial on Fridays throughout the year. In doing this we remember the passion and death of Jesus, and we take on some small portion of his suffering. As St. Paul said, "in my flesh I complete what is lacking in Christ's afflictions for the sake of his body, that is, the Church" (Colossians 1:24).

When Orestes Brownson was alive, the law of the Church required all Catholics to abstain from meat on every Friday of the year. This was the case as late as the 1960s, when Pope Blessed Paul VI allowed bishops to adapt the rule to make it more suitable to local cultures. In places where people rarely eat meat, for example, a fast from meat makes little difference. For a vegetarian or a vegan, the standard Friday abstinence requires no sacrifice at all.

The bishops of the United States permit the faithful to substitute some other pious practice if they do not observe the Friday abstinence from meat. Some people "fast" from their favorite media — television, radio, or portable electronic devices. Some limit their recreational phone calls on Friday.

The important thing is for us to find a fast that's meaningful to us. When we fast, we are clearing away clutter in our life. We are making room for God. We are expressing our earnest expectation that Christ will come to us.

Such fasting should be a regular part of our plan of life, our program of prayer. We should at least observe our Fridays in a distinctive way, in remembrance of the cross of Jesus.

We can and should, however, practice self-denial more often than weekly. We can, for example, leave the last pastry for someone else, even though we would really like to have it ourselves.

We can even fast from complaining, and instead offer up the small daily annoyances and frustrations that come our way. Pope Benedict XVI recommended this practice as a particularly powerful method of prayer and a means to spiritual growth.[21]

Doctors and nutritionists agree that fasting is good for our bodies. A trimmer waistline may be an unexpected benefit of a stronger prayer life, but that's not the reason we fast. Fasting is not dieting. Pope St. John Paul II emphasized this point: "Penitential fasting is obviously something very different from a therapeutic diet, but in its own way it can be considered therapy for the soul. In fact practiced as a sign of conversion, it helps one in the interior effort of listening to God."[22]

We have elsewhere recognized how difficult it can be to "hear" God in our prayer. Well, there is a great saint advising us that fasting can help us to acquire the habit and the skill.

We cannot tune in to God, however, if we are constantly distracted by our material wants and needs and drives and peeves. We all know what happens if we allow ourselves to be dominated by these things. St. Paul spoke of people whose "god is the belly … with minds set on earthly things" (Philippians 3:19). We don't want to live that way.

In fasting we learn to tune out worldly static through self-denial. We learn to let go even of necessities, in the sure knowledge that we "shall not live by bread alone, but by every word that proceeds from the mouth of God" (Matthew 4:4). Again, we learn to defer something good for the sake of something much better.

Self-denial is one way we gain self-mastery. When we fast, we are refusing to let ourselves be ruled by whims, passions, or natural drives. As we grow in self-control, we are better able to love our family members, coworkers, and neighbors. Only when we *possess* ourselves can we truly *give* ourselves in love, as Jesus did.

Fasting, then, like all forms of prayer, is a path to greater love.

CHAPTER 13

The Communion of Saints

God called Dorothy Day to a difficult task.

She was raised in a family that was vaguely Protestant, but irregular about church attendance. Her father was a journalist who changed jobs often, moving his family all over the map, from New York to San Francisco to Chicago. Young Dorothy resented the moves, which prevented her from forming deep friendships. She came to see life as a "long loneliness."

Once, when she was a child, she saw a neighbor woman praying on her knees. Dorothy asked what she was doing, and the woman lifted her beads and explained the Rosary of Our Lady. Little Dorothy took up the practice, praying the beads at bedtime, and it gave her peace, a lasting sense that she was not alone. She sustained her habit of the bedtime Rosary till adolescence, when her thoughts turned to boys and other matters.

Life grew more tumultuous as she entered young adulthood. Moved by the plight of the poor, she dedicated herself to social activism. Her religious sense was weak, however, and she felt increasingly drawn to communism, the workers' movement that was then making inroads throughout the world. She hoped for peaceful revolution that would result in a classless society. Religion she saw as an impediment — "the opiate of the masses," in the words of the philosopher Karl Marx.

Unmoored from religion, Dorothy drifted morally. She was married and divorced. She conceived a child out of wedlock. She had an abortion. She lived with a man she deeply loved.

Still, she felt increasingly lonely, and she realized it was because she desired God. She began to look into the Catholic faith. A friend gave her a set of Rosary beads, and Dorothy remembered the peace she knew as a girl reciting her Hail Marys at bedtime. She took up the practice again, and found herself gripping her beads tightly in her pocket as she went about her daily tasks. She remembered what it was like to have the Blessed Virgin as a companion — and as a mother — and her loneliness receded. Dorothy Day was received into the Catholic Church in 1927.

God had more in store for her. After the Stock Market Crash of 1929, the situation of the poor in the United States became more dire. She began to write about this for the Catholic press, and in 1932 she met an older man named Peter Maurin. He was a visionary and a revolutionary who was steeped in the social teaching of the Catholic Church. With Maurin, Dorothy founded *The Catholic Worker*, which was first a newspaper and then a loosely knit organization. They established "Houses of Hospitality" where the poor could find a meal and the homeless a warm place to sleep.

She had a sense of certainty about her vocation, but it came with a mighty challenge. Dorothy was extremely introverted and had a dread fear of public speaking — yet now, more than ever before, she was invited to give lectures and informal talks. Each time she trembled in terror.

Then a friend, a more experienced Catholic, suggested that Dorothy go to the Blessed Virgin Mary before speaking. Dorothy began doing this, reciting the traditional prayer called the Memorare (Latin for "Remember"). And her fear vanished.

She knew she was not alone. Life was not a long loneliness if its most terrifying moments could be passed in the company of such a mother.

Marian devotion is, without rival, the practice most commonly associated with the "communion of saints." God created us as social beings. It is not good for us to be alone (Genesis 2:18). God made us to depend upon others, and so we live in society.

Society, however, consists of far more than the people we see around us. God's Church is "catholic," and that word means universal. We count as brothers and sisters all of God's children, everywhere in the world. We also know kinship with those who have gone before us and who have died. It is Catholic doctrine that everyone who ever lived, still lives. For God's faithful people, life is changed, not ended. We count as family members the saints in heaven and the faithful who are preparing for heaven through purification in purgatory.

Thus we pray for the dead, especially our family and friends who have passed on. Our relationships don't cease when they have left this life. Though we may have unresolved issues at the time of death, we can still strive to obtain a measure of peace by praying for the dead.

We can also ask the intercession of those whom we know to be in heaven, the saints and blessed ones who have been canonized and beatified by the Church. Though many have lived in faraway lands and long-ago times, they are near to us now in Jesus Christ. They inhabit the same

Church as we do. And when we go to Mass, they are with us. In the penitential rite of the liturgy, we acknowledge the presence of "all the angels and saints."

So, as Catholics, we feel very much at home with the idea of prayer to the saints and the angels. Marian devotion is just about universal. But other saints are popular, too. Catholics tend to call on St. Anthony of Padua for help finding lost items. We turn to St. Francis of Assisi when pets or livestock are ill. We go to St. Jude the Apostle when our deepest needs seem to be "lost causes."

Dorothy Day cultivated many special devotions in the course of her long life. She loved St. Thérèse of Lisieux, also known as the Little Flower, and even wrote a book about her. Dorothy encouraged the children she knew to dress up as their favorite saints on Halloween.

As we read and pray in the Catholic tradition, we will find ourselves attracted to the lives of certain saints. We need not simply strive to *imitate* the saints we admire. We can ask the saints themselves to help us. If they lived next door to us, we would not hesitate to borrow a stick of butter or a lawnmower from them. In a sense, they do live next door to us.

Over time these devotions might develop into lasting supernatural friendship — a special devotion.

We should make a habit also of regular remembrance of our friends and family members who have died. As long as we live, their number grows more numerous. Grieving is a normal part of life, even for Christians who know that life goes on. Life may not be ended, but it is *changed*, and change is often difficult. Prayer for the dead is one way to ease the transition in our relationships. It's one way to manage the change. We mourn — "blessed are those who mourn," Jesus said — but we do so in the sure and certain faith that death does not have the last word. We shall be comforted.

We can make prayer for the dead a regular part of our plan of life. When we think of someone who's passed on, we should take it as a reminder to pray for that person. The traditional Catholic prayer for this purpose is brief:

> Eternal rest grant unto them, O Lord, and let perpetual light shine upon them. May their souls, and the souls of all the faithful departed, through the mercy of God, rest in peace. Amen.

We can also request Masses to be said for the repose of those who have died. We can (sometimes, if we plan far enough in advance) arrange for Masses to be offered on significant anniversaries — a birthday, a wedding anniversary, or the date of their passing.

And we can and should visit the graves of our beloved, if they're nearby. A Catholic cemetery is considered hallowed ground because it holds the remains of the baptized, who still live in Jesus Christ. Like the catacombs in Rome, your local Catholic cemetery can be a place to make pilgrimage and take prayer walks, remembering the souls of the departed as you go.

With every step you can be certain that a Christian never walks alone. A Christian always lives in communion — in a great society that is so much more than the eye can see.

We can make these prayers with confidence because our bonds of communion with those whom we love are not broken in death. Their entrance into eternal life does not end their relationship with us. In a sense, by their passing on to glory, becoming one with God and in God, through the transcendent power of love, we too are somehow brought closer to him.

Our program of prayer should show that we believe all of this.

CHAPTER 14

Alms and Service

Blessed Mother Teresa of Calcutta, in almost seventy years of religious life, tended to many thousands of people. She served the needs of their bodies and the needs of their souls. For twenty years, she did this as an educator. Then, for nearly a half-century, she served the poorest of the poor, especially those who were dying.

She saw her service not so much as a job but as a consequence of her prayer — and even itself a form of prayer. "Every Holy Communion fills us with Jesus and we must, with Our Lady, go in haste to give him to others.... We too, like her, serve others."[23]

Her days were marked by a demanding schedule of prayer and work. As she moved from the chapel to the infirmary, she left Christ to find Christ. In the poor and dying, she said, "I see Jesus Christ in all of his distressing disguises."

Our life of prayer and our life of service are inseparable. If we say we have one and not the other, then we have deluded ourselves. If we don't have charity, we are nothing (see 1 Corinthians 13:1–3).

This is a constant theme in Sacred Scripture. In the Old Testament we read that prayer is good when accompanied by almsgiving. Only "those who perform deeds of charity and of righteousness ... have fullness of life" (Tobit 12:8–9). Prayer and service were, for the people of Israel, like two sides of the same coin: "Do not be fainthearted in your prayer, nor neglect to give alms" (Sirach 7:10). In the New Testament, Cornelius was told: "your prayer has been heard and your alms have been remembered before God" (Acts 10:31).

This is the life the Apostles learned from Jesus. They learned to serve and give alms (Matthew 10:8; 6:2). This is the Gospel they took to the world:

> What does it profit … if a man says he has faith but has not works? Can his faith save him? If a brother or sister is poorly clothed and in lack of daily food, and one of you says to them, "Go in peace, be warmed and filled," without giving them the things needed for the body, what does it profit? So faith by itself, if it has no works, is dead (James 2:14–17).

If we truly desire Jesus — and if we truly seek him in prayer — we will not fail to see him in our neighbors who are in need. Jesus identified himself with the lowliest and neediest of them: "Truly, I say to you, as you did it to one of the least of these my brethren, you did it to me" (Matthew 25:40).

Jesus assumed that we would give alms (see Matthew 6:2–4). But he expects us to share more than we can give by writing a check. He expects us to give ourselves. Pope Francis often speaks of "meeting people who have the greatest need" — and truly *meeting* them. "The important thing," the pope tells us, "is not looking at them from afar, or helping from afar. No, no! It is going to encounter them. This is the Christian! This is what Jesus taught: to go meet the most needy."[24] He urges us to "look into the eyes" of those we serve.

To pray is to seek the face of Jesus, and we can be sure that "everyone … who seeks finds" (Matthew 7:8). But we need to seek him also in the place where he said he could be found, in those who are poor, hungry, homeless, lonely (Matthew 25). When we find Jesus in the poor, then our service itself becomes an act of prayer.

If our prayer is not moving us to greater service, then we are not seeking earnestly enough. If we pray, we will serve. As we pray more, we will find ourselves wanting to serve more. If we are spending more time at prayer and we don't find ourselves growing more charitable, generous, and kind, then we are probably not truly praying.

Prayer and service. Prayer and charity. Prayer and almsgiving. These are inseparable and interdependent. Again, this is the message of Pope Francis:

> A prayer that does not lead you to practical action for your brother — the poor, the sick, those in need of help, a brother in difficulty — is a sterile and incomplete prayer. But, in the same way.... When time is not set aside for dialogue with him in prayer, we risk serving ourselves and not God present in our needy brother and sister.... It is from contemplation, from a strong friendship with the Lord, that the capacity is born in us to live and to bring the love of God, his mercy, his tenderness, to others. And also our work with brothers in need, our charitable works of mercy, lead us to the Lord, because it is in the needy brother and sister that we see the Lord himself.[25]

Biblical faith transforms us so that we can transform the world. In prayer we receive the love of God, and we must share it with the world, or it dies in us.

Some people think that such charity requires us to go to some faraway land to find the destitute. But Blessed Mother Teresa herself corrected that error whenever she encountered it. She said that she found the greatest poverty in the wealthiest nations, where elderly people were often abandoned in institutions to live alone, without visitors and with infrequent phone calls. This kind of poverty — the ache of loneliness — is all around us. It is in even the wealthiest neighborhoods, where parents, spouses, and children are effectively abandoned by people they love. What are we doing about it? Are we telling them, as St. James observed, "Go in peace, be warmed and filled" — yet neglecting to look into their eyes. Are we giving them our time and attention? Are we listening to them? Do we give them our friendship?

An hour given in friendship is not a substitute for prayer. It needs, as the pope pointed out, to be fortified by prayer. But it can itself become a form of prayer. Service is prayer when we know that we are looking into the eyes of Jesus Christ — sometimes in distressing disguise — whenever we look upon those whom we serve.

Service sometimes just happens. We respond spontaneously to an obvious human need. But we should not wait for the opportunity. We need to make time for it. Service must be part of our plan.

CHAPTER 15

An Infinity of Options

In the matter of prayer, we have come through all these chapters, and we have hardly scratched the surface. The Christian tradition is rich. The ways of prayer are many, and as varied as the saints — and the saints are as varied as the people who live in your town or city.

A Catholic who wants to pray can choose from many different devotions; and these devotional practices can eventually, one by one, become building blocks of a plan of life, a program for a personal spirituality, a way of daily living in intimate relationship with God.

In this book we have examined a few broad categories of prayer. There are still more categories, and there are many more forms than could be covered in a short book. If we were to give every form of prayer the discussion it deserves, this book would be at least as large as a dictionary.

Catholics tend to find the ways of prayer that suit them best — suit their circumstances, their cast of mind, their temperament, and their urgent needs. Sometimes these forms are common, and sometimes they are quite unusual.

I know a man who, as soon as he wakes up each day, prays the Gloria from the Mass.

I know a married couple that says devotion to the guardian angels is the way they stay on top of the task of parenting.

I know a doctor who prays a quick prayer to St. Luke, the evangelist and physician, whenever a patient walks into the examining room.

I know people who meditate according to Ignatian methods, and others who follow the classic Carmelite saints Teresa of Ávila and John of the Cross. I know others who pray the Benedictine way.

You will find your way, and you will find it by praying with perseverance.

The Bible preserves a record of spiritual practices that were millennia in the making. In the course of Christian history, these have been further tested and proven — and have found renewed expression — in hundreds of different cultures and in the prayer lives of millions of individuals. These holy souls have influenced a great variety of devotions and left us a seeming infinity of options for our spiritual life.

If I could write that dictionary, I would propose other forms of prayer to you.

Prayer to the Holy Spirit. The third person of the Trinity is the very source and life of our prayer (see Romans 8:13–17 and Galatians 4:6). We receive the Spirit's indwelling at Baptism and pray for growth in the Spirit throughout our lifetime. The traditional form of prayer to the Holy Spirit is very simple: "Come, Holy Spirit!" Catholic tradition works this into many hymns, litanies, and prayers; and these are good for us to know and pray.

Midday prayers. We have mentioned that some people make an examination of conscience at noon. It is also customary to pray a brief sequence of prayers called the Angelus. It takes no more than a couple of minutes, and it's easily remembered because we can associate it with our lunch break. (During Easter Season, the Angelus is replaced by a shorter prayer called the Regina Caeli.)

Sacramentals. These are sacred signs that signify spiritual effects. Some sacramentals are blessings. Others are blessed objects, such as holy water, religious medals, scapulars, holy cards, and sacred images. These provide a physical dimension to our prayer life, reaching the mind and heart through the bodily senses. Sacramentals make us better disposed to receive God's grace.

The Divine Office (also called the **Liturgy of the Hours** or the **Breviary**). This is the Church's official set of daily prayers. Its bedrock is a cycle of Psalms, readings, and canticles from the Bible. Its recitation is mandated for clergy and vowed religious. It has, in recent years, become increasingly popular for laypeople as well.

The Stations of the Cross are a series of fourteen meditations on Jesus' suffering and death. Many parishes pray them publicly on Fridays during Lent. Many individuals pray them on Fridays throughout the year. Great saints and popes have written reflections on the Stations. The papal meditations, usually given on Good Friday in Rome, are available on the Vatican's website.

Annual retreat. This is an extended period of concentrated prayer — perhaps a long weekend, perhaps a week. Retreats can take a wide variety of forms, hosted by monasteries, institutes, or apostolates. These long stretches of relative silence are designed to give us perspective on our spiritual lives.

Devotion to the guardian angels. God has given you a guardian angel, tasked with getting you to heaven by way of a faithful life. It is good for us to "tune in" to the promptings of our holy angel. Many people memorize this simple angel prayer and pray it every day:

> Angel of God, my guardian dear,
> to whom God's love entrusts me here:
> ever this day be at my side
> to light, to guard, to rule, and guide. Amen.

Aspirations. The name comes from the word "breath," and these prayers last hardly longer than the time it takes us to exhale. It is good for us to pray short prayers from Scripture or the liturgy — the lines that stay with us and move our hearts. "Lord, have mercy!" "Thank you!" "Help my unbelief!" "Come to my assistance!" "Lord, that I may see!"

Hymns. Pope St. John Paul II reminded us that to sing is to pray twice, and this is the common doctrine of many saints. It is also our common experience. We've all had moments when hymns sung at Mass have moved us deeply. We can and should sing these hymns when we're alone in the car. We can even listen to them on our MP3 player. This can be prayer.

Again, these few forms — and this whole book — represent just a sampling of the prayer forms that are available to you in the Catholic tradition. If they appeal to you, try them on for a week or more. At first, a particular devotion may seem an ill fit; but give yourself time to grow into it. Don't be quick to abandon a spiritual practice if you don't get the hang of it after a couple of days of trying. Love can't be hurried. Sometimes it takes longer for us to adjust to a new form of prayer.

We should try, too, *not* to add more than one new form of prayer at a time. It's good to concentrate our efforts and get past one hurdle before we try to jump another.

Over the course of months and years, our prayer life will take a shape that is distinctively our own — distinctively yours, distinctively mine. Don't worry if your program of prayer looks different than those of people you know. Your plan will look different, as your life looks different.

St. Paul's plan looked like his life. It included practices he knew from his training as a Pharisee. But it also incorporated the customs of the Catholic Church that was just emerging in history. His program was varied. It included liturgical prayer (1 Corinthians 11), intercession (2 Thessalonians 1:11), pilgrimage (Acts 20:16), thanksgiving (1 Corinthians 1:4), and bodily penance (1 Corinthians 9:27). He prayed with Scripture (1 Timothy 4:5); he prayed alone in the desert of Arabia (Galatians 1:17); and he prayed with others (Acts 20:36). Though he was a very busy man, he prayed constantly (2 Timothy 1:3). What enabled him to do this was God's grace — and his own disciplined response. His prayer was rooted in the religious tradition he had received in childhood, but it was also distinctively his own.

Your prayer will be your own. Through Catholic tradition, God has given you what you need to get started. Now all that remains is for you to pray, one day after another, according to a plan that is entirely yours, yet was God's long before it was yours.

Recommended Reading

Mike Aquilina and Cardinal Donald Wuerl. *The Mass: The Glory, the Mystery, the Tradition*. New York: Image, 2010.

Jordan Aumann, O.P. *Spiritual Theology*. London: Sheed and Ward, 1982. I recommend especially chapters 12 and 13 of this book by my great professor.

Benedict Baur, O.S.B. *In Silence with God*. Princeton, NJ: Scepter, 1997.

Cardinal Joseph Bernardin. *A Game Plan for the Christian*. New Rochelle, NY: Scepter, 1984.

Louis Bouyer. *Introduction to Spirituality*. Collegeville, MN: Liturgical Press, 1961.

Daniel Burke. *Navigating the Interior Life: Spiritual Direction and the Journey to God*. Steubenville, OH: Emmaus Road Press, 2012.

Dom Fernand Cabrol, O.S.B. *The Prayer of the Early Christians*. New York: Benziger Brothers, 1930.

Fr. Walter J. Ciszek, S.J. *He Leadeth Me*. San Francisco: Ignatius Press, 1993.

Congregation for Divine Worship and the Discipline of the Sacraments. *Directory on Popular Piety and the Liturgy: Principles and Guidelines*. Rome: 2001.

Congregation for the Doctrine of the Faith. *Letter to the Bishops of the Catholic Church on Some Aspects of Christian Meditation*. Rome: 1989.

Thomas Dubay, S.M. *Prayer Primer: Igniting a Fire Within*. San Francisco: Ignatius Press, 2002.

Regis Flaherty and Mike Aquilina. *The How-To Book of Catholic Devotions*. Huntington, IN: Our Sunday Visitor, 2000.

St. Francis de Sales. *Introduction to the Devout Life*. New York: Image, 1972.

Romano Guardini. *The Art of Praying: The Principles and Methods of Christian Prayer*. Manchester, NH: Sophia Institute Press, 1994.

Kilian J. Healy, O. Carm. *Awakening Your Soul to the Presence of God: How to Walk with Him Daily and Dwell in Friendship with Him Forever*. Manchester, NH: Sophia Institute Press, 1999.

Gary Jansen. *Exercising Your Soul: Fifteen Minutes a Day to a Spiritual Life*. New York: Hachette, 2010.

Peter Kreeft. *Prayer for Beginners*. San Francisco: Ignatius Press, 2000.

Matthew Leonard. *Prayer Works: Getting a Grip on Catholic Spirituality*. Huntington, IN: Our Sunday Visitor, 2014.

Lawrence G. Lovasik. *The Basic Book of Catholic Prayer: How to Pray and Why*. Manchester, NH: Sophia Institute Press, 1999.

Fr. Thomas G. Morrow. *Be Holy: A Catholic's Guide to the Spiritual Life*. Ann Arbor, MI: Servant Books, 2009.

Michael Scanlan, T.O.R. *Appointment with God*. Bloomingdale, OH: Apostolate for Family Consecration, 1987.

Daria Sockey. *The Everyday Catholic's Guide to the Liturgy of the Hours*. Ann Arbor, MI: Servant Books, 2013.

Cardinal Donald Wuerl. *The Light Is on for You: The Life-Changing Power of Confession*. Frederick, MD: Word Among Us, 2014.

Cardinal Donald Wuerl. *Open to the Holy Spirit: Living the Gospel with Wisdom and Power*. Huntington, IN: Our Sunday Visitor, 2014.

Notes

1 Pope Francis, Homily at Mass, October 8, 2013.

2 Mark K. Shriver, *A Good Man: Discovering My Father, Sargent Shriver* (New York: St. Martin's, 2012), 43.

3 Ibid., 215.

4 Fr. Michael Scanlan, T.O.R., *Appointment with God* (Steubenville, OH: Franciscan University Press, 1987), 15.

5 Monsignor Tran's account of the daily schedule of the papal household was published online, posthumously, by Catholic World News on April 1, 2005. Monsignor Tran died in 2002.

6 Amy Stern, ed., "American Grace: How Religion Divides and Unites Us," transcript of press luncheon, published December 16, 2010 at PewForum.org. Retrieved September 29, 2014.

7 Blessed Mother Teresa of Calcutta, *Where There Is Love, There Is God: A Path to Closer Union with God and Greater Love for Others* (New York: Doubleday, 2012), 20.

8 Jacques Maritain tells the story of his friendship with Satie in the book *Lettre a Jacques Maritain* (Paris: Stock, 1926). Satie's last words are recorded in the diary of Maritain's wife, Raïssa, published in *Jacques et Raïssa Maritain: Oeuvres Complètes*, vol. 15 (Paris: Éditions Saint-Paul, 1995), 321. The translation here is new.

9 This is evident even in the earliest Christian document, titled the *Didache*, which scholars date to the mid-first century.

10 Cath Martin, "Denzel Washington's tips for prayer and gratitude: 'We all fall short, we all got plenty,'" May 27, 2014, ChristianToday.com. Retrieved September 29, 2014.

11 The Scriptures express this reality in the Book of Revelation 1:6; 5:10; 20:6; and in 1 Peter 2:5 and 2:9. The Church's doctrine is especially well stated in the Second Vatican Council's document *Lumen Gentium*, n. 34.

12 Joseph I. Dirvin, *Mrs. Seton* (New York: Avon Books, 1962), 157-158.

13 Ronald Lawler, O.F.M. Cap., "Ordinary Faith in the Eucharist," *Catholic Dossier*, September-October 1996, p. 28.

14 Cardinal Donald Wuerl, *The Light Is On For You: The Life-Changing Power of Confession* (Frederick, MD: Word Among Us, 2014).

15 Pope Francis, Apostolic Exhortation *Evangelii Gaudium*, n. 152.

16 Pope Benedict XVI, Angelus address, November 6, 2005.

17 Pope Francis, Apostolic Exhortation *Evangelii Gaudium*, n. 153.

18 Pope Benedict XVI, "Address to the Participants in the International Congress Organized to Commemorate the 40th Anniversary of the Dogmatic Constitution on Divine Revelation *Dei Verbum*," September 16, 2005.

19 CCC 2709. St. Teresa of Jesus, *The Book of Her Life*, 8,5 in The Collected Works of St. Teresa of Ávila, tr. K. Kavanaugh, O.C.D., and O. Rodriguez, O.C.D. (Washington DC: Institute of Carmelite Studies, 1976) I,67.

20 John Farina, "The Untimid Voice of Orestes Brownson," *Crisis*, October 1986.

21 Pope Benedict XVI, Encyclical Letter *Spe Salvi (Saved in Hope)*, November 30, 2007, n. 40.

22 Pope St. John Paul II, Angelus address, March 10, 1996.

23 Blessed Mother Teresa of Calcutta, Talk to the Brothers and Coworkers of the Missionaries of Charity, Los Angeles, July 1, 1977.

24 Pope Francis, Message to Argentinians, August 7, 2013, www.catholicnewsagency.com.

25 Pope Francis, Angelus address, July 21, 2013.